CHEAT SHEET

SIMPLY FOR

UK

FOODS

✔ Carbohydrate ✔ Glycemic Index ✔ Fiber ✔ Glycemic Load

WITH OVER 390 FOODS BORN IN THE UNITED KINGDOM
OF
GREAT BRITAIN

By

Judith Lickus, B. Sc., LBSW

Published by JML Publishing
Corpus Christi, TX, USA 78404

Notice

This book is a reference to aid in making enlightened selections of foods available in THE UNITED KINGDOM OF GREAT BRITAIN. It is sold with the understanding that the publisher and the author are not liable for the misconception or misuse of any information provided. Every effort has been made to make this book as complete and accurate as possible. The purpose of this book is to educate. The author of *CHEAT SHEET SIMPLY FOR UK FOODS* and its' publisher shall have neither the liability nor responsibility to any person or entity with respect to any loss, damage, or injury caused or alleged to be caused directly or indirectly by the information contained in this book. The information in this book is in no way intended to replace medical advice by a competent health practitioner. This book is not intended as a substitute for any treatment prescribed by your doctor. If you have a medical problem, please see your doctor.

Mention of any particular company, organization, authority, or product manufacturer does not imply endorsement by the author or publisher, nor does mention of any specific company, organization, authority, or product manufacturer imply their endorsement of this book. Specific product information is shown to highlight variations among products, preparation, and manufacturers for the food selection process.

Physical and internet addresses and directions cited in this book were accurate at the time this book went to press.

Copyright © 2017 by Judith Lickus, B. Sc., LBSW

All rights reserved. No part of this publication may be reproduced or transmitted in any form or by any means, graphic, electronic, or mechanical, including photocopying, recording, or by any other information storage and retrieval system, without the written permission of the publisher.

ISBN-13: 978-1547255498

ISBN-10: 1547255498

Published in Corpus Christi, Texas USA by JML Publishing

United Kingdom of Great Britain flag image credit:
https://upload.wikimedia.org/wikipedia/commons/thumb/a/ae/Flag_of_the_United_Kingdom.svg/1200px-Flag_of_the_United_Kingdom.svg.png

Printed by CreateSpace Independent Publishing Platform

OVERVIEW

CHEAT SHEET SIMPLY FOR UK FOODS is set up to streamline the process of locating specific nutrition information for foods grown and produced in the United Kingdom of Great Britain.

There are often huge differences in the same foods originating in different countries. This is true whether the food is a basic fresh produce item such as an apple, orange, or celery, or a manufactured food product.

Basic nutritional content (and often ingredients used) differs from one country to another. This is because different countries have different climates, soil types, growing methods, and even recipes.

Carbohydrate content, glycemic index (GI), and glycemic load (GL) are very dependent upon where a food is grown and how it is prepared or processed. In the case of a manufactured food product, a recipe of the same name, even by the same manufacturer, can vary wildly from one country to another.

International Tables of food nutrition and test study results typically present us with thousands of food entries from countries all over the world. Here you will find a distillation of the important numbers just for foods born in The United Kingdom of Great Britain.

CHEAT SHEET SIMPLY FOR UK FOODS is arranged by glycemic *values*. This pocket guide is built to deliver those food values in a unique way.

Five distinctive food charts create a complete catalog of glycemic values for you. The charts are: Carbohydrate, Glycemic Index, and Glycemic Load, listed low to high. Fibre is listed high to low. In the final list, foods are organized alphabetically by Category. You might find it helpful to insert a small bookmarker or use a sticky note to mark the beginning of each section. Every food includes an average serving size. Each list contains over 390 entries.

CARBOHYDRATE

UNITED KINGDOM OF GREAT BRITAIN foods are catalogued according to the *amount* of carbohydrate they contain, from low to high. The Carbohydrate section organizes the carbohydrate content of foods regardless of their glycemic index, fiber, glycemic load, or category.

Not all carbs are created equal in their effect on metabolism.

The individual *personalities* of carbs are what make all the difference in the world. Those *personalities* are represented by their *glycemic index*.

GLYCEMIC INDEX (GI)

The *personality* of some carbs causes blood glucose to spike. A spike in blood glucose sets off a chain of reactions in the body. A surge of insulin is released, directing the energy into fat cells, while lowering the energy available to blood cells. This lowered available blood cell energy triggers hunger and tiredness, causing metabolism to slow in order to avoid burning energy.

Glycemic index testing began in the scientific community as a way to help diabetics manage their blood glucose levels. Little did the researchers know that their discovery would eventually lead to the root cause of many other diseases as well.

Test subjects fast for 12 hours before testing of a food for glycemic index. For the test, subjects eat a 50 g carb portion of the test food. Their blood glucose is recorded over a two hour period.

A second test is conducted on the same subjects on a different date. Once again, the subjects fast for 12 hours before beginning the test. This time, the subjects consume a 50 g carb portion of pure glucose. Again, blood glucose levels are tested and recorded over a two hour period.

Below is an image showing the results of two human test subjects' blood glucose levels during the first two hours after a meal. The first ate a high GI meal. The second ate a low GI meal. The amount of carbohydrate (50 g) in the meals is the same.

Notice the black arrow (on the lower right of the image). It is pointing to the level of blood glucose at about an hour and a half after the high GI meal. Blood glucose falls to a level that is lower than when the high glycemic meal was eaten.

This is when tiredness, foggy thinking, hunger, and cravings for another high glycemic food can begin to occur.

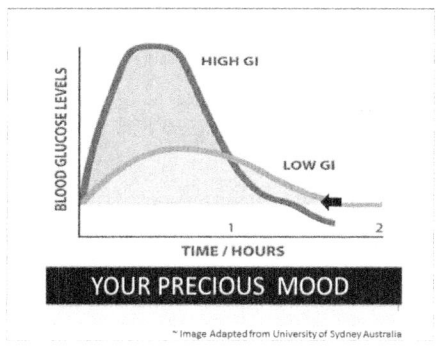

~ Image Adapted from University of Sydney Australia

Scientific study results on the consumption of *high glycemic* carbohydrates point to weight gain, diabetes, heart disease, depression, periodontal disease, poly-cystic ovary disease, and the growth of cancer.

Glycemic index is a blood sugar index, measuring blood glucose levels for the first two hour period during the digestion of a food.

Here is a simple chart for easy reference:

GLYCEMIC INDEX RANKINGS	GLYCEMIC INDEX SCORES
LOW	55 or LESS
INTERMEDIATE (MEDIUM)	56 – 69
HIGH	70 or MORE

To be considered a *low glycemic index* food, a 50g carbohydrate serving must score at 55 or less on a scale of 0 to 100 (with 100 being the measurable reaction to the reference food pure glucose). That means that the low glycemic index food has a glycemic index about half as high as glucose.

A medium glycemic index score is from 56 to 69. And a high glycemic index score is from 70 on up.

The glycemic index scores for food entries presented in *CHEAT SHEET SIMPLY FOR UK FOODS* are the actual test score results of human test subjects by qualified laboratories.

The majority of these test results are based on 50g carbohydrate portions. A few additional entries are included only when both the test food and the reference food contain the same amount of carbohydrate. The GI results shown are those simply for United Kingdom of Great Britain specific foods.

Foods are listed by their glycemic index (GI) score from low to high. The Glycemic Index section organizes foods regardless of carbohydrate, fiber, glycemic load, or category.

FIBRE

Fibre only comes from plant foods. Fibre creates bulk throughout the entire digestion process, slowing down the movement of food through the stomach and small intestine. Foods that are rich in fiber keep you feeling full longer, and your blood glucose stable.

In The United Kingdom of Great Britain, fibre is analyzed using two different methods. The first method is the Englyst method. In the Englyst method, fibre that is resistant to digestion is removed from the food samples and only the remaining non-starch polysaccharides (NSP) are included in the resulting fibre count.

In the second method, designed by the Association of Official Analytical Chemists (AOAC), all fibre, even that which is resistant to digestion, is included in the fibre count.

The results reported by the Department of Health Survey (DH) include fibre counts for BOTH the Englyst and the AOAC methods. The results of the DH Survey are published in the *Composition of Foods Integrated Dataset* and *McCance and Widdowson's The Composition of Foods* series.

It is not the intent of either testing method to measure the glycemic index of any food, just the fibre content. The problem is that some of the food samples used in BOTH of these dual testing procedures had been previously frozen for a year.

The fact is that freezing a food *does* affect its' *personality*. That *personality* is, of course, measurable by *glycemic index* testing. It is a top priority in a book of nutritional values to report fibre counts with regard to glycemic index. In terms of glycemic index testing, freezing a food for a year qualifies as a *preparation method*.

As you will see when you review the food charts, many previously *frozen* foods have been clinically tested (on human subjects) and given a glycemic index score. Some if these results can be quite remarkable.

Have you ever noticed how different a previously frozen fruit or vegetable looks and tastes compared to fresh?

Our primary focus is to report the fibre content of the entire edible portion in the *natural state* of the food -- that has not been frozen for a year. The United States Department of Agriculture (USDA) offers such a fibre resource. The USDA resource uses the AOAC method of reporting fiber (which includes both the soluble and insoluble fibre.) Therefore the USDA provides fibre counts in *CHEAT SHEET SIMPLY FOR UK FOODS*.

In this book, whenever a previously frozen sample was used for glycemic index testing, the FOOD description clearly states that fact.

Foods are organized in the fibre chart according to their fibre content from the highest to the lowest amount of fibre in a typical serving. The Fibre section organizes foods regardless of carbs, glycemic index, glycemic load, or category.

GLYCEMIC LOAD (GL)

While glycemic index is mainly an accurate measure of the *personality* of individual carbs, glycemic load represents a combination of the number of carbs and their own personal glycemic index. Current medical research reveals that the glycemic load is the most trustworthy basis in natural blood sugar regulation.

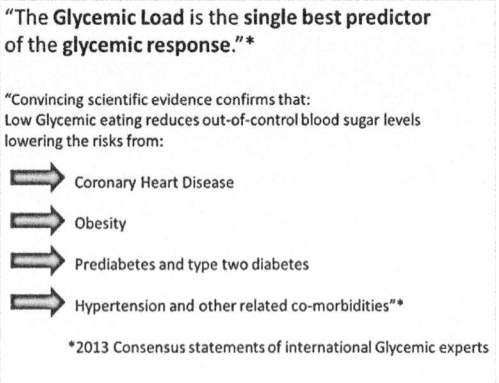

"The **Glycemic Load** is the **single best predictor** of the **glycemic response.**"*

"Convincing scientific evidence confirms that:
Low Glycemic eating reduces out-of-control blood sugar levels lowering the risks from:

⟹ Coronary Heart Disease

⟹ Obesity

⟹ Prediabetes and type two diabetes

⟹ Hypertension and other related co-morbidities"*

*2013 Consensus statements of international Glycemic experts

Here is a simple chart of glycemic load scores for easy reference:

GLYCEMIC LOAD RANKINGS	GLYCEMIC LOAD SCORES
LOW	10 or LESS
INTERMEDIATE (MEDIUM)	11 – 19
HIGH	20 or GREATER

Glycemic load (GL) is calculated this way:

GI X Carbs /100 = GL.

To better understand the benefit of Glycemic Load we will compare two carbohydrate foods.

We will look at 30 g serving of a slice of white bread and a slice of a package cake mix with frosting.

First, we will judge these foods by a count of their carbs.
Next, we will compare the glycemic index of the two foods.
Finally, we will calculate the glycemic load of each of them. This will show us, gram for gram, which one has the least effect on blood glucose levels.

CARB COUNTING

Here we have a slice of bread, and a slice of frosted cake.
Both of these foods are 30 g servings.
First, we will compare the number of carbs in a 30 g serving:

The bread has 14 g carbs
The cake has 17 g carbs.

 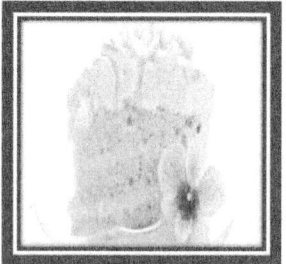

By counting carbs alone, the bread would be the best choice.

Many think that counting carbs is the only thing that matters for weight loss and blood glucose control. It is commonly thought that we need a certain amount of carbs to turn into glucose for our brain. That's because they think that carbs are the only nutrient that is converted into glucose. But that is simply not true.

The good news is that our bodies convert protein and fat into glucose whenever there is a glucose shortage.

Back to our example:

GLYCEMIC INDEX

Now we will look at glycemic index (GI).

The GI of the bread is 70.
The GI of the cake is 42.

 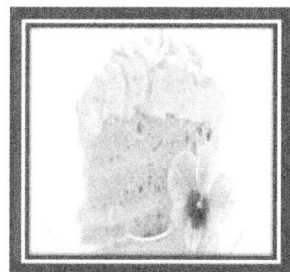

By using the GI alone, the cake is the best choice.

The truth is that we are making a comparison to discover the lesser of two evils in order to demonstrate the use of a scientific principal.

In reality, neither one of these foods has much real *nutritional* value. What we are seeing is how a principal works in real life, in terms of blood glucose control.

And so back to our example, the bread has less carbs than the cake, but the cake has a lower glycemic index than the bread. How do we decide which one will raise our blood glucose less?

Let's look at what the glycemic load has to say:

GLYCEMIC LOAD

Now we will calculate glycemic load.

Bread: 14 g carbs X 70 (GI) = 980 / 100 = 9.80 (10)

Cake: 16 g carbs X 42 (GI) = 658 / 100 = 6.58 (7)

 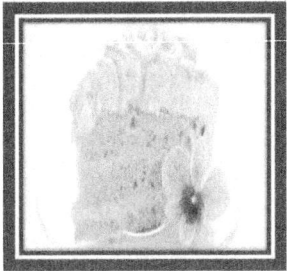

As you can see, the Queen was right when she said, "Let them eat cake."

So, there it is ... the 30 g of frosted cake actually comes out better than the 30 g of white bread for blood glucose control because it actually has a *lower glycemic load* score.

But, you may say, "Bread is the staff of life!" Bread is economical, and some types of bread (mainly non-white types) do provide nutrition. Selection is a tricky process. Stable blood glucose levels are at risk.

Many health professionals consider GI and GL too "complex" to use. That translates into not listing glycemic values on packaged products and not including these scores in national nutrient database files.

So it is up to the consumer to figure it out.

This pocket guide is built to provide glycemic values for foods in the United Kingdom of Great Britain. Since it is possible to review refined *country-specific* data, it may be possible to decide if *using* these food *facts* is worth it to you or not.

Before we move on, we will look at one more example of calculating glycemic load:

Simply Carb Counting V.S. Using GI

50g. Corn tortilla	50g. Wheat tortilla
Carbs = 24	Carbs = 26
GI = 52	GI = 30
Here's the math:	Here's the math:
52 X 24 = 1248	30 X 26 = 780
1248/100 = 12.48 GL	780/100 = 7.80 GL

Based on the carbs, the corn tortilla has the lowest number. If you were just carb counting, you would select the corn tortilla. Based in the GI, the wheat tortilla has the lowest score. When the glycemic load is calculated, we find that the wheat tortilla is the better choice.

See how easy it is to calculate the glycemic load when you know the glycemic index and the number of carbs in a serving of food? The glycemic index stays the same no matter the amount of food or grams of carbs. The number of carbs changes based on the serving size.

The key in both examples happens to be a lower glycemic index. The key could just as easily be less carbs. Going with a smaller portion size will lower glycemic load, too.

CHEAT SHEET SIMPLY FOR UK FOODS provides detailed scientific test results that include specifics of how to prepare and serve bread (and many other high glycemic foods) for a low glycemic index (GI) and a low glycemic load (GL).

Foods are listed according to their Glycemic Load (GL) score, from low to high. The Glycemic Load section organizes foods by their glycemic load ranking, regardless of carbs, glycemic index, fiber or category.

ALPHABETICALLY BY CATEGORY

In the final list, all foods are organized alphabetically into the following nineteen categories:

Bakery, Beverages, Bread, Cereal, Convenience Meals, Dairy, Fish-Meat-Poultry, Fruit, Grain, Infant Foods, Meal Replacement & Weight Management, Nuts, Pasta, Pulses, Snacks, Soup, South American, Sweetener, and Vegetable.

In the Category section, it is easiest to compare different varieties of the same types of foods.

In the dairy category, yoghurt is a noteworthy section. You will find that there are 42 tested yoghurts listed in these charts. Glycemic Load scores for these yoghurts range from 1 all the way up to 30!

The Category section organizes foods into their groups regardless of carbs, glycemic index, fiber or glycemic load.

ABOUT CARBOHYDRATE METABOLISM

The charts in this book are specifically organized to serve as a reference guide for selecting foods based on factors that affect carbohydrate metabolism and blood glucose levels.

Bookmarking the beginning of each food chart might be useful.

Listing carbohydrate, glycemic index and glycemic load from low to high displays foods at the top of the charts that have a very minimal impact on blood glucose levels. Fibre, both soluble and insoluble, also helps to regulate blood sugar levels. Displaying high-fibre foods at the top of the Fibre chart makes it simple to find foods that will increase the amount of fibre in the diet. This provides a straightforward catalogue of foods with the least glycemic impact. Many make great snacking ideas, too.

When you *substitute* these foods (toward the top of the charts) for others (toward the bottom of the charts), these foods will keep you feeling full longer and keep blood glucose levels stable. The more of these foods you add to your plate, the more they *displace* other foods with a higher glycemic load that spike blood glucose levels and require larger amounts of insulin to digest.

As the final list, "Category," organizes entries into their food groups, an opportunity presents itself to discover various *preparation* and *serving methods* and the effect they have on carbohydrate metabolism and blood glucose levels. These preparation and serving methods are detailed, and the nutritional values (Carbs, GI, Fibre, serving size, and GL) are listed.

The word "/Special" is included in the category column to make these entries stand out from the others. They are grouped together in the Category section.

In many cases, just a simple treatment turns a high GI food into a low GI food. Lowering the GI of a food can lower the GL of the serving. Lowering the GL of a serving can have a powerful effect on blood glucose levels.

Of particular benefit are various preparation and serving methods for bread, cereal, grain, pasta, and the potato. Such easy techniques have a powerful impact on the glycemic index (GI), and glycemic load (GL) of carbohydrates.

ೞಲ

TABLE OF CONTENTS

OVERVIEW
CARBOHYDRATE
GLYCEMIC INDEX (GI)
FIBRE
GLYCEMIC LOAD (GL)
ALPHABETICALLY BY CATEGORY
ABOUT CARBOHYDRATE METABOLISM

CARBOHYDRATE	1
GLYCEMIC INDEX (GI)	25
FIBRE	49
GLYCEMIC LOAD (GL)	73
CATEGORY	97
ENDNOTES, REFRENCES & RESOURCES	119

Low G-i
All good

CARBOHYDRATE

CARBOHYDRATE

REF#	CATEGORY	FOOD	GI	SERV	UM	CARB	FIBRE	GL
USDA	Beverage	Coffee or tea, black, unsweetened	0			0	0	0
USDA	Beverage	Seltzer water, baking extract flavored, stevia sweetened	0			0	0	0
USDA	Beverage	Water	0			0	0	0
G/USDA	Meat, Fish & Poultry	All meat, fish, shellfish, poultry, including wild game or meats	0			0	0	0
G/USDA	Snack	Sardines, fish snacks, canned	0	95	g	0	0	0
PKG	Sweetener	Stevia extract	0			0	0	0
G	Beverage	Beer, wine, spirits (no GI, but can have carbs, depending on brand)	0			0		
G/USDA	Snack	Dill Pickle	40	28	g	0.6	0.3	0
G/PKG	Beverage	Coconut Milk, unsweetened	0	240	mL	1	0	0
G/USDA	Beverage	Almond Milk, unsweetened	0	226	mL	1	1	0
G/USDA	Vegetable	Radish	40	30	g	1	1	0
G/USDA	Snack	Egg, hardboiled	0		g	1	0	0
PKG	Sweetener	Stevia	0	1	g	<1	0	0
G/USDA	Vegetable	Watercress	40	120	g	2	1	1
PKG	Sweetener	Xylitol (1 packet)	7	2.04	g	2	0	0
G/USDA/#	Fruit	Strawberries	40	120	g	3	2	1
G/USDA/#	Pulses	Cocoa powder, unsweetened	40	5	g	3	1	1
G/USDA	Vegetable	Spinach	0	150	g	4	3	0
H/USDA	Snack	Hummus, chickpea salad dip, commercially prepared	6	30	g	4	2	0
G/USDA	Vegetable	Green Leaf Lettuce	0	150	g	4	2	0

Low g-1
ALL good

CARBOHYDRATE

REF#	CATEGORY	FOOD	GI	SERV	UM	CARB	FIBRE	GL
G/USDA	Vegetable	Arugula	40	120	g	4	2	2
G/USDA	Vegetable	Celery	40	120	g	4	2	2
G/USDA	Vegetable	Swiss chard	40	120	g	4	2	2
G/USDA	Vegetable	Cucumber	40	120	g	4	1	2
G/USDA	Vegetable	Mushrooms	40	120	g	4	1	2
G/USDA	Vegetable	Zucchini	40	120	g	4	1	2
G/USDA	Dairy	Creamed cottage cheese	30	226	g	4	0	1
PKG	Sweetener	Coconut palm sugar	35	4	g	4	0	1
PKG	Sweetener	Coconut palm sugar	35	4	g	4	0	1
G/USDA	Vegetable	Asparagus	40	120	g	5	3	2
USDA/#	Pulses	Carob powder, unsweetened	40	6	g	5	2	2
G/USDA/#	Fruit	Rhubarb	40	120	g	5	2	2
G/USDA	Vegetable	Ginger root	40	28	g	5	1	2
G/USDA	Vegetable	Radiccio	40	120	g	5	1	2
G/USDA	Vegetable	Tomato	40	120	g	5	1	2
G/USDA	Vegetable	Collard greens	40	120	g	6	5	2
G/USDA	Vegetable	Cauliflower	40	120	g	6	2	2
G/USDA	Vegetable	Mustard greens	40	120	g	7	9	3
G/USDA	Nuts	Pecans	0	50	g	7	5	0
G/USDA	Nuts	Macadamia	0	50	g	7	4	0
G/USDA	Nuts	Walnuts	0	50	g	7	4	0
G/USDA	Vegetable	Eggplant	40	120	g	7	4	3
G/USDA	Vegetable	Kohlrabi	40	120	g	7	4	3
G/USDA/	Vegetable	Olives	40	120	g	7	4	3

Low g-l
All good

CARBOHYDRATE

REF#	CATEGORY	FOOD	GI	SERV	UM	CARB	FIBRE	GL
#								
G/USDA	Snack	Celery with Hummus	40	80	g	7	3	0
G/USDA	Vegetable	Cabbage	40	120	g	7	3	3
G/USDA	Vegetable	Tomatillo	40	120	g	7	2	3
G/USDA	Vegetable	Bok Choy	40	120	g	7	1	3
B752	Dairy	Fromage Frais, red fruit: blackcurrant Healthy Living, (UK)	22	100	g	7		2
B754	Dairy	Fromage Frais, red fruit: red cherry (UK)Healthy Living,	25	100	g	7		2
B755	Dairy	Fromage Frais, red fruit: strawberry, Healthy Living, (UK)	29	100	g	7		2
B756	Dairy	Fromage Frais, yellow fruit: mandarin and orange, Healthy Living, (UK)	19	100	g	7		1
B757	Dairy	Fromage Frais, yellow fruit: mango and papaya, Healthy Living, (UK)	25	100	g	7		2
B758	Dairy	Fromage Frais, yellow fruit: passionfruit and pineapple, Healthy Living, (UK)	18	100	g	7		1
B759	Dairy	Fromage Frais, yellow fruit: peach and apricot, Healthy Living, (UK)	22	100	g	7		1
G/USDA	Nuts	Hazelnuts	0	50	g	8	5	0
G/USDA	Vegetable	Green Beans	40	120	g	8	4	3
G/USDA	Vegetable	Okra	40	120	g	8	4	3
G/USDA	Vegetable	Broccoli	40	120	g	8	3	3
G/USDA/#	Fruit	Figs	40	28	g	8	1	3
G/USDA	Vegetable	Garlic	40	28	g	8	1	3

CARBOHYDRATE

REF#	CATEGORY	FOOD	GI	SERV	UM	CARB	FIBRE	GL
G/USDA	Bakery	Cookie, Ranger Cookies, (From recipe in Are You Sweet Enough Already?)	35	80	g	9	10	3
B1067	Infant Foods	Creamed rice porridge, Robinsons first Tastes from 4 months, Nutricia, Wells, (UK)	59	75	g	9		5
A447.2	Infant foods	Creamed porridge, Robinsons First Tastes from 4 months, Nutricia Wells (UK)	59	75	g	9		5
G/USDA	Vegetable	Grape leaves	40	60	g	10	7	4
G/USDA	Snack	Celery with Cashew Butter	40	80	g	10	2	2
G/USDA/#	Fruit	Cantaloupe	40	120	g	10	1	4
B267	Bread	Multigrain bread, Sainsbury's, (UK)	80	30	g	10		8
B1320	Nuts	Cashew nut halves (UK)	27	50	g	10		3
B1321	Nuts	Cashew nuts, roasted and salted (UK)	27	50	g	10		3
B1599	Sweetener	Lactose, 25 g portion, DBH, Poole, (UK)	48	10	g	10		5
A591.1	Sweetener	25 g Litesse II bulking agent with polydextrose and sorbitol (by weight), Danisco Sweeteners UK) vs 25 g carb in ref food (glucose).	7	10	g	10		1
A591.2	Sweetener	25 g Litesse III ultra bulking agent with polydextrose and sorbitol (by weight), Danisco Sweeteners UK) vs 25 g carb in ref food (glucose).	4	10	g	10		0
A593.3	Sweetener	25 g Xylitol (by weight), Danisco Sweeteners UK) vs ref food with 25 g. carb (glucose). Mean of 2 studies	8	10	g	10		1
G/USDA	Fruit	Avocado	0	120	g	11	8	0

CARBOHYDRATE

REF#	CATEGORY	FOOD	GI	SERV	UM	CARB	FIBRE	GL
G/USDA/#	Fruit	Rose hips	40	28	g	11	7	4
G/USDA	Nuts	Almond meal flour	0	50	g	11	6	0
G/USDA	Nuts	Almonds	0	50	g	11	6	0
G/USDA	Vegetable	Jicama	40	120	g	11	6	4
G/USDA	Vegetable	Dandelion greens	40	120	g	11	4	4
H/USDA	Snack	Microwave popcorn plain, average	55	20	g	11	3	6
G/USDA	Vegetable	Bell pepper	40	120	g	11	2	4
G/USDA	Vegetable	Kale	40	120	g	11	2	4
G/USDA	Vegetable	Onion	40	120	g	11	2	4
G/USDA/#	Fruit	Honeydew	40	120	g	11	1	4
B234	Bread	Wholemeal whole wheat, wheat flour bread Hovis, (UK)	68	30	g	11		7
B236	Bread	Wholemeal whole wheat, wheat flour bread Sainsbury's,(UK)	71	30	g	11		8
B239	Bread	Wholemeal whole wheat, wheat flour bread Hovis, (UK)	74	30	g	11		8
B278	Bread	Seeded bread (UK)	49	30	g	11		6
B474	Cereal	Breakfast Cereal bar, hazelnut flavor (UK)	33	30	g	11		4
B1068	Infant Foods	Rice pudding, Robinsons first Tastes from 4 months, Nutricia, Wells, (UK)	59	75	g	11		6
A447.3	Infant foods	Rice pudding, Robinsons First Tastes from 4 months (Nutricia Wells UK)	59	75	g	11		6
G/USDA	Snack	Chocolado Parfait with a Cherry, (From recipe in Are You Sweet Enough Already?)	40	113	g	12	6	5

CARBOHYDRATE

REF#	CATEGORY	FOOD	GI	SERV	UM	CARB	FIBRE	GL
G/USDA/#	Fruit	Blackberries	0	120	g	12	4	0
G/USDA	Vegetable	Beet greens	40	120	g	12	3	5
G/USDA/#	Fruit	Mulberries	40	120	g	12	2	5
B111	Bread	Barley, Sunflower and barley bread Vogel's, (UK), course 80% kernels	70	30	g	12		8
B184	Bread	White wheat flour flour bread Hovis Classic, British Bakeries Ltd, (UK)	87	30	g	12		11
B189	Bread	White wheat flour bread, fresh, toasted British Bakeries Ltd, (UK)	63	40	g	12		8
B245	Bread	Wholemeal flour, stoneground whole wheat, Waitrose,(UK)	66	30	g	12		8
B273	Bread	Multiseed bread (UK)	54	30	g	12		7
B191	Bread/Spec.	White wheat flour bread, frozen and defrosted British Bakeries Ltd, (UK)	75	30	g	12		9
B193	Bread/Spec.	White wheat flour bread, frozen, defrosted and toasted, British Bakeries Ltd, (UK)	64	30	g	12		8
B200	Bread/Spec.	White wheat flour bread with added wheatgerm and fiber with oat fiber (UK) (Italy)	59	30	g	12		6
B312	Cereal	Bran cereal, high fiber (UK)	43	30	g	12		5
B787	Dairy	Milk, Full-fat, pasteurised, fresh, organic, Arla, (UK)	34	250	mL	12		4
B789	Dairy	Milk, Full-fat, standardised homogenised, pasteurised, British Dairycrest, (UK)	46	250	mL	12		5
B843	Dairy/Yoghurt	Yoghurt, black cherry, Healthy Living Light, (UK)	67	200	g	12		8

CARBOHYDRATE

REF#	CATEGORY	FOOD	GI	SERV	UM	CARB	FIBRE	GL
B853	Dairy/Yoghurt	Yoghurt, red fruit: Morello cherry, Healthy Living Light, (UK)	35	200	g	12		4
B861	Dairy/Yoghurt	Yoghurt, summer fruit: raspberry, Healthy Living Light, (UK)	28	200	g	12		3
B864	Dairy/Yoghurt	Yoghurt, tropical fruit: guava and passionfruit, Healthy Living Light, (UK)	24	200	g	12		3
B1318	Nuts	Cashew nuts (UK)	25	50	g	12		3
B1319	Nuts	Cashew nuts, organic, roasted and salted (UK)	25	50	g	12		3
G/USDA	Vegetable	Artichoke	40	120	g	13	6	5
G/USDA/#	Fruit	Apricot	40	120	g	13	2	5
G/USDA/#	Fruit	Papaya	40	120	g	13	2	5
G/USDA/#	Fruit	Plum	40	120	g	13	2	5
PKG	Sweetener	Blackstrap molasses	55	15	mL	13	0	7
B1128	Pulses	Split peas, yellow, dried, soaked overnight, boiled 55 min (UK)	25	150	g	13		3
B172	Bread	White flour (UK)	59	30	g	13		8
B187	Bread	White wheat flour bread, homemade (UK)	89	30	g	13		12
B190	Bread	White wheat flour bread, homemade, fresh, toasted (UK)	66	40	g	13		9
B190.1	Bread/Spec.	White wheat flour bread, toasted, mean of three studies	60	30	g	13		8
B256	Bread	Crusty malted wheat bread, Finest, (UK)	52	30	g	13		7
A78.1	Bread	Gluten-free fiber-enriched bread, unsliced gluten-free wheat starch soya bran) (UK)	69	30	g	13		9
A78.2	Bread	Gluten-free fiber-enriched bread, sliced gluten-free wheat starch soya bran (UK)	76	30	g	13		10

CARBOHYDRATE

REF#	CATEGORY	FOOD	GI	SERV	UM	CARB	FIBRE	GL
A78.3	Bread	Gluten-free fiber-enriched bread, Mean of 2 studies	73	30	g	13		9
B194	Bread/Spec.	White wheat flour bread, homemade, frozen, defrosted	54	30	g	13		7
B228	Bread/Spec.	White bread, prepared with a 10 min prove and a second 2 min proving low loaf volume) (UK)	38	30	g	13		5
B229	Bread/Spec.	White bread, prepared with a 30 min prove and a second 12 min proving moderate loaf volume (UK)	72	30	g	13		9
B230	Bread/Spec.	White bread, prepared with a 60 min prove and a second 30 min proving moderate loaf volume (UK)	86	30	g	13		11
B231	Bread/Spec.	White bread, prepared with a 40 min prove, a second 25 min proving and a third 50 min proving large loaf volume (UK)	100	30	g	13		13
B192	Bread/Spec.	White wheat flour bread, homemade, frozen and defrosted (UK)	62	30	g	13		8
B753	Dairy	Fromage Frais, red fruit: raspberryHealthy Living, (UK)	31	100	g	13		2
B796	Dairy	Milk, semi-skimmed, British Dairycrest, (UK)	25	250	mL	13		3
B797	Dairy	Milk, semi-skimmed, pasteurised, organic Arla, (UK)	34	250	mL	13		4
B818	Dairy	Milk, skimmed, pasteurised, British Dairycrest, (UK)	48	250	mL	13		6
B854	Dairy/Yoghurt	Yoghurt, red fruit: raspberry and black cherry, Healthy Living Light, (UK)	37	200	g	13		5
B859	Dairy/Yoghu	Yoghurt, summer fruit:	11	200	g	13		1

CARBOHYDRATE

REF#	CATEGORY	FOOD	GI	SERV	UM	CARB	FIBRE	GL
	rt	apricot, Healthy Living Light, (UK)						
B860	Dairy/Yoghurt	Yoghurt, summer fruit: peach and vanilla, Healthy Living Light, (UK)	26	200	g	13		3
B862	Dairy/Yoghurt	Yoghurt, summer fruit: strawberry, Healthy Living Light, (UK)	36	200	g	13		5
B865	Dairy/Yoghurt	Yoghurt, tropical fruit: mango, Healthy Living Light, (UK)	32	200	g	13		4
B866	Dairy/Yoghurt	Yoghurt, tropical fruit: peach and apricot, Healthy Living Light, (UK)	27	200	g	13		3
B867	Dairy/Yoghurt	Yoghurt, tropical pineapple, Healthy Living Light, (UK)	38	200	g	13		5
B1066	Infant Foods	Apple, apricot and banana cereal, Robinsons first Tastes from 4 months, Nutricia, Wells, (UK)	56	75	g	13		7
A447.1	Infant foods	Apple apricot and banana cereal6, Robinsons First Tastes from 4 months, Nutricia Wells, (UK)	56	75	g	13		11
PKG	Sweetener	Blackstrap molasses	55	15	mL	13	0	7
G/USDA/#	Fruit	Biosenberries	40	120	g	14	6	0
G/USDA/#	Fruit	Cranberries	40	120	g	14	6	6
G/USDA/#	Fruit	Cherries, red	40	120	g	14	2	6
B175	Bread	White wheat flour bread, Sainsbury's, (UK)	70	30	g	14		10
B268	Bread	Multigrain batch bread (UK)	62	30	g	14		9
B296	Bread	Pita bread, unleavened, wholemeal (UK)	56	30	g	14		8
B475	Cereal	Breakfast Cereal bar, orange flavor (UK)	33	30	g	14		5
B842	Dairy/Yoghu	Yoghurt, black cherry,	17	200	g	14		2

CARBOHYDRATE

REF#	CATEGORY	FOOD	GI	SERV	UM	CARB	FIBRE	GL
	rt	Finest, (UK)						
B869	Dairy/Yoghurt	Yoghurt, vanilla, Healthy Living Light, (UK)	47	200	g	14		7
B744	Snack	Crackers, Wholewheat sticks, crunchy, yeast extract flavored (UK)	50	25	g	14		7
G/USDA	Fruit	Raspberries	0	120	g	15	8	3
B676	Bakery	Cookie, Oat biscuit (UK)	45	25	g	15		7
B149	Bread	Oatmeal batch bread (UK)	62	30	g	15		9
B180	Bread	White wheat flour bread, Hovis, (UK)	73	30	g	15		11
B183	Bread	White wheat flour bread, Hovis, (UK)	75	30	g	15		11
B188	Bread	White wheat flour bread, toasted, Hovis, (UK)	50	41	g	15		7
B295	Bread	Pita bread, unleavened, white, mini (UK)	68	30	g	15		10
A77.1	Bread	Gluten-free white bread gluten-free wheat starch (UK), Unsliced	71	30	g	15		11
A77.2	Bread	Gluten-free white bread gluten-free wheat starch) (UK), Sliced	80	30	g	15		12
A77.3	Bread	Gluten-free white bread gluten-free wheat starch (UK), Mean of 2 studies	76	30	g	15		11
A356	Bread	Rye crispbread, High-fiber rye crispbread Ryvita Company Ltd Poole Dorset (UK)	59	25	g	15		9
B1270	Bread/Spec.	White bread 30 g, toasted, served with cheddar cheese 36 g, Hovis, (UK)	35	66	g	15		5
B473	Cereal	Breakfast Cereal bar, cranberry flavor (UK)	42	30	g	15		6
B1173	Con. Meal	Beef and ale casserole, convenience meal Finest, (UK)	53	300	g	15		8
B743	Snack	Crackers, Wholewheat with pumpkin and thyme (UK)UK)	36	25	g	15		6
B1412	Snack	Apricot and Almond bar	34	30	g	15		5

CARBOHYDRATE

REF#	CATEGORY	FOOD	GI	SERV	UM	CARB	FIBRE	GL
		(UK)						
G/USDA	Vegetable	Wheatgrass	40	30	g	16	8	6
G/USDA/#	Fruit	Pineapple	40	120	g	16	2	3
G/USDA/#	Fruit	Mandarin	40	120	g	16	2	7
G/USDA/#	Fruit	Tangerine	40	120	g	16	2	7
B135	Bread	Fruit and cinnamon bread, Finest, (UK)	71	30	g	16		11
B137	Bread	Fruit loaf, sliced (UK)	57	30	g	16		9
B852	Dairy/Yoghurt	Yoghurt, raspberry, Healthy Living Light, (UK)	43	200	g	16		7
B857	Dairy/Yoghurt	Yoghurt, strawberry, Healthy Living Light, (UK)	30	200	g	16		5
B863	Dairy/Yoghurt	Yoghurt, toffee, Healthy Living Light, (UK)	41	200	g	16		7
B630	Digestive	Digestives (UK)	39	25	g	16		6
B1322	Nuts	Mixed nuts and raisins (UK)	21	50	g	16		3
B716	Snack	Crackers, Choice grain (UK)	49	25	g	16		8
B733	Snack	Crackers, Rye with oats (UK)	64	25	g	16		10
B734	Snack	Crackers, Rye with sesame (UK)	57	25	g	16		9
B742	Snack	Crackers, Wholegrain with sesame seeds and rosemary (UK)	53	25	g	16		8
B1642	Vegetable	Potato, Nicola, peeled, quartered, boiled 15 min (UK)	59	150	g	16		9
G/USDA/#	Fruit	Guava	40	120	g	17	6	7
G/USDA	Fruit	Blueberries	29	120	g	17	3	5
G/USDA	Vegetable	Leek	40	120	g	17	2	7
B342	Cereal	High-fiber cereal (UK)	52	30	g	17		9
B751	Dairy	Crème fraiche dessert, raspberry, Finest, (UK)	30	150	g	17		5

CARBOHYDRATE

REF#	CATEGORY	FOOD	GI	SERV	UM	CARB	FIBRE	GL
B850	Dairy/Yoghurt	Yoghurt, peach & apricot, Healthy Living Light, (UK)	28	200	g	17		5
A318	Digestive	Digestives gluten-free, maize starch, Nutricia Dietary Care Ltd Redish Stockport (UK)	58	25	g	17		10
B1323	Nuts	Mixed nuts, roasted and salted (UK)	24	50	g	17		4
G/USDA	Vegetable	Turmeric root	40	28	g	18	6	7
G/USDA	Pulses	Chickpea (Garbanzo Bean) flour	10	30	g	18	5	2
G/USDA/#	Fruit	Kiwi	40	120	g	18	4	6
G/USDA/#	Fruit	Mango	40	120	g	18	2	7
B699	Bakery	Cookie, Rich Tea (UK)	40	25	g	18		7
B1115	Pulses	Lentils, red, split, dried, boiled 25 min (UK)	21	150	g	18		4
A356	Bread	Rye crispbread Ryvita Company Ltd (UK)	63	25	g	18		11
B363	Cereal	Muesli, fruit and nut (UK)	59	30	g	18		11
B376	Cereal	Muesli, wholewheat (UK)	56	30	g	18		10
B1131	Meal Repl. & Weight Mgmt.	Chocolate weight management drink (UK)	23	250	mL	18		4
B1132	Meal Repl. & Weight Mgmt.	Chocolate weight management drink (UK)	39	250	mL	18		7
B1540	Soup	Chicken and mushroom soup (UK)	46	250	g	18		8
B1557	Soup	Vegetable soup (UK)	60	250	g	18		11
G/USDA	Bakery	Chocolate Black Bean Cake (From recipe in Are You Sweet Enough Already?)	40	80	g	19	4	8
B355	Cereal	Muesli, Alpen original, made from steamed rolled oats with dried fruit and nuts, Weetabix, (UK)	55	30	g	19		11
B359	Cereal	Muesli, Value, UK)	64	30	g	19		12
B462	Cereal/Spec.	Muesli, Original, Sainsbury's, (UK),	60	30	g	19		11

CARBOHYDRATE

REF#	CATEGORY	FOOD	GI	SERV	UM	CARB	FIBRE	GL
		consumed with semi-skimmed milk						
B463	Cereal/Spec.	Muesli, Swiss, Sainsbury's, (UK), consumed with semi-skimmed milk	60	30	g	19		12
B464	Cereal/Spec.	Muesli, Wheat free, Pertwee Farm's, (UK), consumed with semi-skimmed milk	49	30	g	19		9
B1129	Meal Repl. & Weight Mgmt.	Chocolate, lactose-free, weight management drink (UK)	29	250	mL	19		6
B1541	Soup	Chicken and mushroom soup (UK)	69	250	g	19		13
G/USDA/#	Fruit	Soursop	40	120	g	20	4	2
G/USDA/#	Fruit	Lychee	40	120	g	20	2	4
B1090	Pulses	Butter Beans, dried, soaked overnight, boiled 50 min (UK)	26	150	g	20		5
B313	Cereal	Branflakes, Healthy Living, (UK)	50	30	g	20		10
B334	Cereal	Fruit and Fibre, Value, (UK)	68	30	g	20		13
B441	Cereal	Wheat based cereal biscuit (UK) (Plain flaked wheat)	72	30	g	20		14
B449	Cereal/Spec.	Branflakes, Sainsbury's, (UK), with semi-skimmed milk	76	30	g	20		15
B265	Bread	Malt loaf, organic (UK)	59	30	g	21		12
B1269	Bread/Spec.	White bread 30 g, toasted, served with baked Beans, 51 g, Hovis, (UK)	50	81	g	21		11
B332	Cereal	Fruit and Fibre™, Sainsbury's, UK)	61	30	g	21		13
B333	Cereal	Fruit and Fibre (UK)	67	30	g	21		14
B334.1	Cereal	Fruit and Fibre, mean of three studies	65	30	g	21		13
B353	Cereal	Mini Wheats, whole wheat, Sainsbury's, (UK)	59	30	g	21		12
B361	Cereal	Muesli, Healthy Eating, (UK)	86	30	g	21		18
B362	Cereal	Muesli, fruit (UK)	67	30	g	21		14
B1146	Meal Repl. & Weight Mgmt.	Lemon weight management bar (UK)	32	50	g	21		7
A142	Bread	Whole-wheat snack bread, Ryvita Co Ltd Poole Dorset (UK)	74	30	g	22		16
B465	Cereal/Spec.	Porridge, jumbo oats (UK)Sainsbury's, UK),	40	250	g	22		9

CARBOHYDRATE

REF#	CATEGORY	FOOD	GI	SERV	UM	CARB	FIBRE	GL
		consumed with semi-skimmed milk						
B466	Cereal/Spec.	Porridge, small oats, Sainsbury's, (UK), consumed with semi-skimmed milk	61	250	g	22		14
B951	Fruit	Apricots, dried, ready to eat (UK)	31	60	g	22		7
B952	Fruit	Apricots, dried, ready to eat, bite size (UK)	32	60	g	22		7
B1008	Fruit	Peach, dried (UK)	35	60	g	22		8
G/USDA/#	Fruit	Pomegranate	40	120	g	23	9	2
G/USDA	Snack	Apple slices with peanut butter	38	120	g	23	5	9
G/USDA	Snack	Apple slices with peanut butter	38	120	g	23	5	9
B304	Cereal	Balance™, Sainsbury's, (UK)	74	30	g	23		17
B455	Cereal/Spec.	Hot oat cereal, 30 g, cocoa flavor (UK) prepared with 125 mL skim milk	40	155	g	23		9
B459	Cereal/Spec.	Hot oat cereal 30 g prepared with 125 mL skim milk	47	155	g	23		11
B460	Cereal/Spec.	Hot oat cereal, 30 g prepared with 125 mL skim milk (UK)	40	155	g	23		9
B1188	Con. Meal	Chow mein, chicken, convenience meal, Healthy Living, (UK)	55	300	g	23		13
B750	Dairy	Crème fraiche dessert, peach, Finest, (UK)	28	150	g	23		7
B1149	Meal Repl. & Weight Mgmt.	SlimFast® chocolate meal replacement bar SlimFast Foods Ltd, UK)	27	50	g	23		6
B1634	Vegetable	Potato, Charlotte, peeled, quartered, boiled 15 min (UK)	66	150	g	23		15
B1635	Vegetable	Potato, Charlotte, boiled (UK)	81	150	g	23		19
B1680	Vegetable	Potato, New, boiled (UK)	80	150	g	23		18
A744/USDA	South American	Corn tortilla (Mexican)	52	50	g	24	1	12
B1111	Pulses	Red Kidney Beans, dried, soaked overnight, boiled 60 min (UK)	51	150	g	24		12
B460.1	Cereal/Spec.	Cereal, Hot oat cereal mean of seven foods prepared with 125 mL skim milk	46	155	g	24		11

CARBOHYDRATE

REF#	CATEGORY	FOOD	GI	SERV	UM	CARB	FIBRE	GL
B467	Cereal/Spec.	Precise, Sainsbury's, (UK), with semi-skimmed milk	59	30	g	24		14
B1147	Meal Repl. & Weight Mgmt.	Malt toffee weight management bar (UK)	43	50	g	24		10
B1410	Snack	Fruit and nut mix, Finest, (UK)	15	50	g	24		4
G/USDA	Fruit	Banana, slightly under-ripe, yellow with green sections	42	120	g	25	3	11
B325	Cereal	Cornflakes, Kellogg's, (UK)	93	30	g	25		23
B452	Cereal/Spec.	Cornflakes, Sainsbury's, (UK) 30 g, consumed with 125 mL skim milk	65	30	g	25		16
B456	Cereal/Spec.	Hot oat cereal, 30 g, fruit flavor (UK) prepared with 125 mL skim milk	47	155	g	25		12
B458	Cereal/Spec.	Hot oat cereal 30 g, orchard fruit flavor (UK) prepared with 125 mL skim milk	5	155	g	25		12
B468	Cereal/Spec.	Rice Pops™, Sainsbury's, (UK), with semi-skimmed milk	80	30	g	25		20
A749/USDA	South American	Wheat tortilla (Mexican)	30	50	g	26	5	8
B454	Cereal/Spec.	Hot oat cereal 30 g, berry flavor (UK) prepared with 125 mL skim milk	43	155	g	26		11
B457	Cereal/Spec.	Hot oat cereal, 30 g, honey flavor (UK), prepared with 125 mL skim milk	47	155	g	26		12
B472	Cereal/Spec.	Wheat Cereal biscuit 30 g, wheat based, consumed with 125 mL skim milk (UK)	47	155	g	26		12
B1253	Con. Meal	Steak and ale with cheddar mash potato convenience meal, Finest, (UK)	48	300	g	26		12
B1637	Vegetable	Potato, Estima, peeled, quartered, boiled 15 min (UK)	66	150	g	26		17
B1651	Vegetable	Potato, white, boiled (UK)	96	150	g	26		24
B1672	Vegetable	Potato, Desiree, mashed (UK)	102	150	g	26		26
B1674	Vegetable	Potato, Estima, microwaved 6 min then baked 10 min (UK)	93	150	g	26		24
B1227	Vegetable/Spec.	Potato, Estima, 50 g, microwaved 6 min then baked 10 min, served with canned tuna, 62 g (UK)	76	112	g	26		20

CARBOHYDRATE

REF#	CATEGORY	FOOD	GI	SERV	UM	CARB	FIBRE	GL
B1228	Vegetable/Spec.	Potato, Estima, 50 g, microwaved 6 min then baked 10 min, served with cheddar cheese 62 g (UK)	39	112	g	26		10
B469	Cereal/Spec.	Wheat Cereal biscuit 30 g, cocoa flavor, consumed with 125 mL skim milk (UK)	46	155	g	27		12
B470	Cereal/Spec.	Wheat Cereal biscuit 30 g, fruit flavor, consumed with 125 mL skim milk (UK)	56	155	g	27		15
B471	Cereal/Spec.	Wheat Cereal biscuit 30 g, honey flavor, consumed with 125 mL skim milk (UK)	52	155	g	27		14
B472.1	Cereal/Spec.	Wheat Cereal biscuit, consumed with 125 mL skim milk, mean of four foods	50	155	g	27		13
B1205	Con. Meal	Lamb moussaka, prepared convenience meal, Finest, (UK)	35	300	g	27		10
B855	Dairy/Yoghurt	Yoghurt, red fruit: raspberry and cranberry, Healthy Living Light, (UK)	42	200	g	27		11
B1012	Fruit	Pear, dried (UK)	43	60	g	27		12
B1153	Meal Repl. & Weight Mgmt.	SlimFast® Garden vegetable soup with peppers and croutons, SlimFast Foods Ltd, UK)	20	250	mL	27		5
B1543	Soup	Garden vegetable soup with peppers and croutons, SlimFast®, SlimFast Foods Ltd, Slough, Berks, UK)	20	250	g	27		5
B1627	Vegetable	Potato, white, baked with skin, baked (UK)	69	150	g	27		19
B1630	Vegetable	Potato, white, baked without skin, baked (UK)	98	150	g	27		26
USDA/#	Fruit	Passionfruit	40	120	g	28	12	5
B451	Cereal/Spec.	Cocoa Crunch cereal 30 g with 125 mL skim milk (UK)	58	155	g	28		16
B881	Dairy/Yoghurt	Yoghurt, Low-fat, apricot (UK)	42	200	g	28		12
B882	Dairy/Yoghurt	Yoghurt, Low-fat, black cherry (UK)	41	200	g	28		11
B884	Dairy/Yoghurt	Yoghurt, Low-fat, peach melba, Value, (UK)	56	200	g	28		16
B885	Dairy/Yoghurt	Yoghurt, Low-fat, raspberry (UK)	34	200	g	28		10
B558	Grain/Spec.	Rice, Basmati, white, boiled 12 min, Value, (UK)	52	150	g	28		15

CARBOHYDRATE

REF#	CATEGORY	FOOD	GI	SERV	UM	CARB	FIBRE	GL
B558	Grain/Spec.	Rice, Basmati, white, boiled 12 min, Value, (UK)	52	150	g	28		15
B1499	Snack	Tropical fruit and nut mix, Finest, UK)	49	50	g	28		14
B1639	Vegetable	Potato, King Edward potato, peeled, quartered, boiled 15 min in unsalted water (UK)	75	150	g	28		21
B1048	Beverage	Cranberry juice drink, Ocean Spray®, Gerber Ltd., Bridgewater, Somerset, (UK)	56	250	mL	29		16
A39	Beverage	Cranberry juice drink Ocean Spray, Gerber Ltd Bridgewater (UK)	56	250	mL	29		16
A402	Beverage	Cranberry juice drink, Ocean Spray; Gerber Ltd Bridgewater Somerset(UK)	56	250	mL	29		16
B397	Cereal	Porridge, organic, made from rolled oats (UK)	63	250	g	29		18
B450	Cereal/Spec.	Cereal flakes with fruit (UK)30 g), consumed with 125 mL skim milk (UK)UK)	57	155	g	29		16
B883	Dairy/Yoghurt	Yoghurt, Low-fat, hazelnut (UK)	53	200	g	29		15
B908	Dairy/Yoghurt	Yoghurt, probiotic, prune (UK)	44	200	g	29		13
B909	Dairy/Yoghurt	Yoghurt, probiotic, raspberry (UK)	45	200	g	29		13
B910	Dairy/Yoghurt	Yoghurt, probiotic, strawberry (UK)	52	200	g	29		15
B910.1	Dairy/Yoghurt	Yoghurt, probiotic, mean of three foods	47	200	g	29		14
B1641	Vegetable	Potato, Maris Piper, peeled, quartered, boiled 15 min in unsalted water (UK)	85	150	g	29		25
B396	Cereal	Porridge made from rolled oats, Value, UK)	63	250	g	30		19
B453	Cereal/Spec.	Honey Crunch cereal 30 g, consumed with 125 mL skim milk (UK)	54	155	g	30		16
B1209	Con. Meal	Lasagne, type NS (UK)	25	300	g	30		8
B886	Dairy/Yoghurt	Yoghurt, Low-fat, strawberry (UK)	61	200	g	30		18
B1152	Meal Repl. & Weight Mgmt.	SlimFast® Strawberry Supreme ready-to-drink shake, SlimFast Foods Ltd, UK)	33	250	mL	30		10

CARBOHYDRATE

REF#	CATEGORY	FOOD	GI	SERV	UM	CARB	FIBRE	GL
B398	Cereal	Porridge, made from rolled oats, Scottish (UK)	63	250	g	31		20
B1195	Con. Meal	Cumberland fish pie (UK)	40	300	g	31		12
B1208	Con. Meal	Lasagne, type NS, Finest, (UK)	34	300	g	31		10
B919	Dairy/Yoghurt	Yoghurt, Probiotic drink, cranberry (UK)	56	250	mL	31		17
B921	Dairy/Yoghurt	Yoghurt, Probiotic drink, original (UK)	34	250	mL	31		11
B1229	Vegetable/Spec.	Potato, Estima 50 g, microwaved 6 min then baked 10 min, served with chilli con carne, 63 g (UK)	75	113	g	31		23
B844	Dairy/Yoghurt	Yoghurt, bourbon vanilla, Finest, (UK)	64	200	g	32		20
B847	Dairy/Yoghurt	Yoghurt, Greek style, honey topped (UK)	36	200	g	32		12
B851	Dairy/Yoghurt	Yoghurt, peach melba, Value, (UK)	57	200	g	32		18
B870	Dairy/Yoghurt	Yoghurt, white peach, Finest, (UK)	54	200	g	32		17
B1150	Meal Repl. & Weight Mgmt.	SlimFast® Chocolate Muesli snack bar, SlimFast Foods Ltd, UK)	49	50	g	32		16
B1640	Vegetable	Potato, Marfona, peeled, quartered, boiled 15 min in unsalted water (UK)(UK)	56	150	g	32		18
B868	Dairy/Yoghurt	Yoghurt, Valencia orange, Finest, (UK)	34	200	g	33		11
B1148	Meal Repl. & Weight Mgmt.	SlimFast® chocolate caramel meal replacement bar, SlimFast Foods Ltd, Slough, Berks, UK)	54	50	g	33		18
B1194	Con. Meal	Cottage pie (UK)	65	300	g	34		22
B846	Dairy/Yoghurt	Yoghurt, Devonshire fudge, Finest, (UK)	37	200	g	34		13
B920	Dairy/Yoghurt	Yoghurt, Probiotic drink, orange (UK)	30	250	mL	34		10
B1154	Meal Repl. & Weight Mgmt.	SlimFast® Pasta Florentina meal, SlimFast Foods, UK)	53	250	g	34		12
B1654	Vegetable/Spec.	Potato, Type NS, boiled in salted water, refrigerated, reheated, India)	23	150	g	34		8
B1206	Con. Meal	Lasagne, beef, frozen (UK)	47	300	g	35		17
B895	Dairy/Yoghurt	Yoghurt, low fat, natural (UK)	35	200	g	35		12

CARBOHYDRATE

REF#	CATEGORY	FOOD	GI	SERV	UM	CARB	FIBRE	GL
B411	Cereal	Porridge, Instant oat cereal porridge prepared with water (UK)	83	250	g	36		30
B1196	Con. Meal	Cumberland pie (UK)	29	300	g	37		11
B524	Grain	Long grain, white, pre-cooked, microwaved 2 min, Express Rice, plain, Uncle Ben's, Masterfoods, (UK)	52	150	g	37		19
A280	Grain	Long grain white precooked microwaved 2 min, Express Rice plain Uncle Ben's; King's Lynn Norfolk (UK)	52	150	g	37		19
B1226	Vegetable/Spec.	Potato, Estima, 50 g, microwaved 6 min then baked 10 min, served with baked beans, 89 g, (UK)	62	139	g	37		23
G/USDA/#	Fruit	Plantain	40	120	g	38	3	10
B1189	Con. Meal	Chow mein, chicken, convenience meal, Serves One, (UK)	47	300	g	38		18
B1207	Con. Meal	Lasagne, meat, Healthy Living, chilled, (UK)	28	300	g	38		11
B845	Dairy/Yoghurt	Yoghurt, champagne rhubarb, Finest, (UK)	49	200	g	38		19
B858	Dairy/Yoghurt	Yoghurt, strawberry and cream, Finest, (UK)	41	200	g	38		16
B1264	Bread/Spec.	White bread roll with cheese (UK)	50	100	g	40		20
B1249	Con. Meal	Sausages and mash potato, prepared convenience meal (UK)	61	300	g	40		25
B849	Dairy/Yoghurt	Yoghurt, orange blossom, Finest, (UK)	42	200	g	40		17
B856	Dairy/Yoghurt	Yoghurt, Scottish raspberry, Finest, (UK)	32	200	g	40		13
B559	Grain/Spec.	Rice, Basmati, white, organic, boiled 10 min (UK)	57	150	g	40		23
B562	Grain/Spec.	Rice, Basmati, white, boiled 8 min (UK)	69	150	g	40		28
G/USDA/#	Fruit	Persimmon	40	120	g	41	4	4
B992	Fruit	Mixed fruit, dried, Value, (UK)	60	60	g	41		24
B564	Grain	Rice, Basmati, easy-cook rice, boiled, Sainsbury's, (UK)	68	150	g	41		28

CARBOHYDRATE

REF#	CATEGORY	FOOD	GI	SERV	UM	CARB	FIBRE	GL
B565	Grain	Rice, Precooked basmati rice in pouch, white, reheated in microwave, Uncle Ben's Express® Masterfoods, (UK)	57	150	g	41		24
A297	Grain	Precooked basmati rice in pouch white reheated in microwave, Uncle Ben's Express; Masterfoods. Kings Lynn Norfolk (UK)	57	150	g	41		24
B1334	Pasta	Fusilli pasta twists, wholewheat, dry pasta, boiled 10 min in unsalted water (UK)	55	180	g	41		23
A24	Beverage	Lucozade original, sparkling glucose drink) Glaxo Wellcome Ltd Uxbridge UK)	95	250	mL	42		40
B1200	Con. Meal	Fajitas, chicken (UK)	42	300	g	42		18
B1030	Fruit	Sultanas, Value, (UK)	56	60	g	42		23
B1031	Fruit	Sultanas (UK)	58	60	g	42		24
B492	Grain	Barley, pearled, boiled 60 min (UK)	35	150	g	42		15
B563	Grain/Spec.	Rice, Basmati, easy cook, white, boiled 9 min (UK)	67	150	g	42		28
B1335	Pasta	Gluten-free pasta, maize starch, boiled 8 min (UK)	54	180	g	42		23
A522	Pasta	Gluten-free pasta maize starch boiled 8 min (UK)	54	180	g	42		22
B1214	Con. Meal	Lasagne, Mushroom stroganoff with rice (UK)	26	300	g	43		11
B1216	Con. Meal	Lasagne, Pasta bake, tomato and mozzarella (UK)	23	300	g	43		10
B557	Grain	Rice, Basmati, white, boiled, Sainsbury's, (UK)	43	150	g	43		18
B1342	Pasta	Lasagne, egg, dry pasta, boiled in unsalted water for 10 min(UK)	53	180	g	43		23
B1251	Con. Meal	Shepherds pie, prepared convenience meal (UK)	66	300	g	44		29
B1383	Pasta	Tagliatelle, egg pasta, boiled in water for 7 min (UK)	46	180	g	44		20
B1384	Pasta	Tagliatelle, egg, boiled, Sainsbury's, UK)	54	180	g	44		24
B848	Dairy/Yoghurt	Yoghurt, lemon curd, Finest, (UK)	67	200	g	45		30

CARBOHYDRATE

REF#	CATEGORY	FOOD	GI	SERV	UM	CARB	FIBRE	GL
B1333	Pasta	Fusilli pasta twists, tricolour, dry pasta, boiled 10 min in unsalted water (UK)	51	180	g	45		23
B1343	Pasta	Lasagne, egg, verdi, dry pasta, boiled in unsalted water for 10 min (UK)	52	180	g	45		23
B1343.1	Pasta	Lasagne, egg, verdi, boiled in unsalted water for 10 min, mean of three studies	53	180	g	45		24
B1186	Con. Meal	Chilli beef noodles, prepared convenience meal, Finest, (UK)	42	300	g	46		19
B532	Grain	Rice, American, easy-cook rice, Sainsbury's, (UK)	49	150	g	46		22
B1151	Meal Repl. & Weight Mgmt.	SlimFast® Double Chocolate meal replacement powder, prepared with skim milk, SlimFast Foods Ltd, UK)	36	50	g	46		17
B1334.1	Pasta	Fusilli pasta, twists, mean of four studies	55	180	g	46		25
B1341	Pasta	Lasagne sheets, dry pasta, boiled in unsalted water for 10 min, Value, UK)	55	180	g	47		26
B1181	Con. Meal	Chicken korma and peshwari rice, prepared meal,Finest, UK)	44	300	g	48		21
B1182	Con. Meal	Chicken korma and rice, convenience meal, Healthy Living, (UK)	45	300	g	48		21
B1210	Con. Meal	Lasagne, vegetarian (UK)	20	300	g	48		10
B1331	Pasta	Fusilli pasta twists, Tesco Stores Ltd, UK), boiled 10 min in salted water (UK)	61	180	g	48		29
B1332	Pasta	Fusilli pasta twists, dry pasta, boiled in 10 min in unsalted water (UK)	54	180	g	48		26
B1217	Pasta/Spec.	Fusilli pasta twists, Tesco Stores Ltd, UK), boiled 10 min in salted water, served with canned tuna (UK)	28			48		13
B1218	Pasta/Spec.	Fusilli pasta twists, Tesco Stores Ltd, UK), boiled 10 min in salted water, served with cheddar cheese (UK)	27			48		13
B1219	Pasta/Spec.	Fusilli pasta twists, Tesco Stores Ltd, UK), boiled 10 min in salted water, served with chilli con carne (UK)	40			48		19

CARBOHYDRATE

REF#	CATEGORY	FOOD	GI	SERV	UM	CARB	FIBRE	GL
B1257	Con. Meal	Sweet and sour chicken with noodles, prepared convenience meal, Serves One, (UK)	41	300	g	52		21
B1180	Con. Meal	Cannelloni, spinach and ricotta (UK)	15	300	g	54		8
B1185	Con. Meal	Chicken tikka masala and rice, convenience meal, Healthy Living, (UK)	34	300	g	60		21
B1258	Con. Meal	Tandoori chicken masala & rice convenience meal, Finest, (UK)	45	300	g	61		27

CARBOHYDRATE

CARBOHYDRATE

GLYCEMIC INDEX (GI)

REF#	CATEGORY	FOOD	GI	SERV	UM	CARB	FIBRE	GL
USDA	Beverage	Coffee or tea, black, unsweetened	0			0	0	0
USDA	Beverage	Seltzer water, baking extract flavored, stevia sweetened	0			0	0	0
USDA	Beverage	Water	0			0	0	0
G/USDA	Meat, Fish & Poultry	All meat, fish, shellfish, poultry, including wild game or meats	0			0	0	0
G/USDA	Snack	Sardines, fish snacks, canned	0	95	g	0	0	0
PKG	Sweetener	Stevia extract	0			0	0	0
G	Beverage	Beer, wine, spirits (no GI, but can have carbs, depending on brand)	0			0		
PKG	Sweetener	Stevia extract	0			0	0	0
G/PKG	Beverage	Coconut Milk, unsweetened	0	240	mL	1	0	0
G/USDA	Beverage	Almond Milk, unsweetened	0	226	mL	1	1	0
G/USDA	Snack	Egg, hardboiled	0		g	1	0	0
G/USDA	Vegetable	Spinach	0	150	g	4	3	0
G/USDA	Vegetable	Green Leaf Lettuce	0	150	g	4	2	0
G/USDA	Nuts	Pecans	0	50	g	7	5	0
G/USDA	Nuts	Macadamia	0	50	g	7	4	0
G/USDA	Nuts	Walnuts	0	50	g	7	4	0
G/USDA	Nuts	Hazelnuts	0	50	g	8	5	0
G/USDA	Fruit	Avocado	0	120	g	11	8	0
G/USDA	Nuts	Almond meal flour	0	50	g	11	6	0
G/USDA	Nuts	Almonds	0	50	g	11	6	0
G/USDA/#	Fruit	Blackberries	0	120	g	12	4	0

GLYCEMIC INDEX (GI)

REF#	CATEGORY	FOOD	GI	SERV	UM	CARB	FIBRE	GL
G/USDA	Fruit	Raspberries	0	120	g	15	8	3
PKG	Sweetener	Stevia	0	1	g	<1	0	0
A591.2	Sweetener	25 g Litesse III ultra bulking agent with polydextrose and sorbitol (by weight,), Danisco Sweeteners UK) vs 25 g carb in ref food (glucose).	4	10	g	10		0
B458	Cereal/Spec.	Hot oat cereal 30 g, orchard fruit flavor (UK) prepared with 125 mL skim milk	5	155	g	25		12
H/USDA	Snack	Hummus, chickpea salad dip, commercially prepared	6	30	g	4	2	0
PKG	Sweetener	Xylitol (1 packet)	7	2.04	g	2	0	0
A591.1	Sweetener	25 g Litesse II bulking agent with polydextrose and sorbitol (by weight), Danisco Sweeteners UK) vs 25 g. carb in ref food (glucose).	7	10	g	10		1
A593.3	Sweetener	25 g Xylitol (by weight), Danisco Sweeteners UK) vs ref food (glucose) with 25 g. carb. Mean of 2 studies	8	10	g	10		1
G/USDA	Pulses	Chickpea (Garbanzo Bean) flour	10	30	g	18	5	2
B859	Dairy/Yoghurt	Yoghurt, summer fruit: apricot, Healthy Living Light, (UK)	11	200	g	13		1
B1410	Snack	Fruit and nut mix, Finest, UK)	15	50	g	24		4
B1180	Con. Meal	Cannelloni, spinach and ricotta (UK)	15	300	g	54		8
B842	Dairy/Yoghurt	Yoghurt, black cherry, Finest, (UK)	17	200	g	14		2
B758	Dairy	Fromage Frais, yellow fruit: passionfruit and pineapple, Healthy Living, (UK)	18	100	g	7		1
B756	Dairy	Fromage Frais, yellow fruit: mandarin and orange, Healthy Living, (UK)	19	100	g	7		1

GLYCEMIC INDEX (GI)

REF#	CATEGORY	FOOD	GI	SERV	UM	CARB	FIBRE	GL
B1153	Meal Repl. & Weight Mgmt.	SlimFast® Garden vegetable soup with peppers and croutons, SlimFast Foods Ltd, UK)	20	250	mL	27		5
B1543	Soup	Garden vegetable soup with peppers and croutons, SlimFast®, SlimFast Foods Ltd, Slough, Berks, UK)	20	250	g	27		5
B1210	Con. Meal	Lasagne, vegetarian (UK)	20	300	g	48		10
B1322	Nuts	Mixed nuts and raisins (UK)	21	50	g	16		3
B1115	Pulses	Lentils, red, split, dried, boiled 25 min (UK)	21	150	g	18		4
B752	Dairy	Fromage Frais, red fruit: blackcurrant Healthy Living, (UK)	22	100	g	7		2
B759	Dairy	Fromage Frais, yellow fruit: peach and apricot, Healthy Living, (UK)	22	100	g	7		1
B1131	Meal Repl. & Weight Mgmt.	Chocolate weight management drink (UK)	23	250	mL	18		4
B1654	Vegetable/Spec.	Potato, Type NS, boiled in salted water, refrigerated, reheated, India)	23	150	g	34		8
B1216	Con. Meal	Lasagne, Pasta bake, tomato and mozzarella (UK)	23	300	g	43		10
B864	Dairy/Yoghurt	Yoghurt, tropical fruit: guava and passionfruit, Healthy Living Light, (UK)	24	200	g	12		3
B1323	Nuts	Mixed nuts, roasted and salted (UK)	24	50	g	17		4
B754	Dairy	Fromage Frais, red fruit: red cherry (UK)Healthy Living,	25	100	g	7		2
B757	Dairy	Fromage Frais, yellow fruit: mango and papaya, Healthy Living, (UK)	25	100	g	7		2
B1318	Nuts	Cashew nuts (UK)	25	50	g	12		3
B1319	Nuts	Cashew nuts, organic, roasted and salted (UK)	25	50	g	12		3
B1128	Pulses	Split peas, yellow, dried, soaked overnight, boiled 55 min (UK)	25	150	g	13		3
B796	Dairy	Milk, semi-skimmed,	25	250	mL	13		3

GLYCEMIC INDEX (GI)

REF#	CATEGORY	FOOD	GI	SERV	UM	CARB	FIBRE	GL
		British Dairycrest, (UK)						
B1209	Con. Meal	Lasagne, type NS (UK)	25	300	g	30		8
B860	Dairy/Yoghurt	Yoghurt, summer fruit: peach and vanilla, Healthy Living Light, (UK)	26	200	g	13		3
B1090	Pulses	Butter Beans, dried, soaked overnight, boiled 50 min (UK)	26	150	g	20		5
B1214	Con. Meal	Lasagne, Mushroom stroganoff with rice (UK)	26	300	g	43		11
B1320	Nuts	Cashew nut halves (UK)	27	50	g	10		3
B1321	Nuts	Cashew nuts, roasted and salted (UK)	27	50	g	10		3
B866	Dairy/Yoghurt	Yoghurt, tropical fruit: peach and apricot, Healthy Living Light, (UK)	27	200	g	13		3
B1149	Meal Repl. & Weight Mgmt.	SlimFast® chocolate meal replacement bar SlimFast Foods Ltd, UK)	27	50	g	23		6
B1218	Pasta/Spec.	Fusilli pasta twists, Tesco Stores Ltd, UK), boiled 10 min in salted water, served with cheddar cheese (UK)	27			48		13
B861	Dairy/Yoghurt	Yoghurt, summer fruit: raspberry, Healthy Living Light, (UK)	28	200	g	12		3
B850	Dairy/Yoghurt	Yoghurt, peach & apricot, Healthy Living Light, (UK)	28	200	g	17		5
B750	Dairy	Crème fraiche dessert, peach, Finest, (UK)	28	150	g	23		7
B1207	Con. Meal	Lasagne, meat, Healthy Living, chilled, (UK)	28	300	g	38		11
B1217	Pasta/Spec.	Fusilli pasta twists, Tesco Stores Ltd, UK), boiled 10 min in salted water, served with canned tuna (UK)	28			48		13
B755	Dairy	Fromage Frais, red fruit: strawberry, Healthy Living, (UK)	29	100	g	7		2
G/USDA	Fruit	Blueberries	29	120	g	17	3	5
B1129	Meal Repl. & Weight Mgmt.	Chocolate, lactose-free, weight management drink (UK)	29	250	mL	19		6

GLYCEMIC INDEX (GI)

REF#	CATEGORY	FOOD	GI	SERV	UM	CARB	FIBRE	GL
B1196	Con. Meal	Cumberland pie (UK)	29	300	g	37		11
G/USDA	Dairy	Creamed cottage cheese	30	226	g	4	0	1
B857	Dairy/Yoghurt	Yoghurt, strawberry, Healthy Living Light, (UK)	30	200	g	16		5
B751	Dairy	Crème fraiche dessert, raspberry, Finest, (UK)	30	150	g	17		5
A749/USDA	South American	Wheat tortilla (Mexican)	30	50	g	26	5	8
B920	Dairy/Yoghurt	Yoghurt, Probiotic drink, orange (UK)	30	250	mL	34		10
B753	Dairy	Fromage Frais, red fruit: raspberryHealthy Living, (UK)	31	100	g	13		2
B951	Fruit	Apricots, dried, ready to eat (UK)	31	60	g	22		7
B865	Dairy/Yoghurt	Yoghurt, tropical fruit: mango, Healthy Living Light, (UK)	32	200	g	13		4
B1146	Meal Repl. & Weight Mgmt.	Lemon weight management bar (UK)	32	50	g	21		7
B952	Fruit	Apricots, dried, ready to eat, bite size (UK)	32	60	g	22		7
B856	Dairy/Yoghurt	Yoghurt, Scottish raspberry, Finest, (UK)	32	200	g	40		13
B474	Cereal	Breakfast Cereal bar, hazelnut flavor (UK)	33	30	g	11		4
B475	Cereal	Breakfast Cereal bar, orange flavor (UK)	33	30	g	14		5
B1152	Meal Repl. & Weight Mgmt.	SlimFast® Strawberry Supreme ready-to-drink shake, SlimFast Foods Ltd, UK)	33	250	mL	30		10
B787	Dairy	Milk, Full-fat, pasteurised, fresh, organic, Arla, (UK)	34	250	mL	12		4
B797	Dairy	Milk, semi-skimmed, pasteurised, organic Arla, (UK)	34	250	mL	13		4
B1412	Snack	Apricot and Almond bar (UK)	34	30	g	15		5
B885	Dairy/Yoghurt	Yoghurt, Low-fat, raspberry (UK)	34	200	g	28		10
B1208	Con. Meal	Lasagne, type NS, Finest, (UK)	34	300	g	31		10
B921	Dairy/Yoghurt	Yoghurt, Probiotic drink, original (UK)	34	250	mL	31		11
B868	Dairy/Yoghurt	Yoghurt, Valencia	34	200	g	33		11

GLYCEMIC INDEX (GI)

REF#	CATEGORY	FOOD	GI	SERV	UM	CARB	FIBRE	GL
		orange, Finest, (UK)						
B1185	Con. Meal	Chicken tikka masala and rice, convenience meal, Healthy Living, (UK)	34	300	g	60		21
PKG	Sweetener	Coconut palm sugar	35	4	g	4	0	1
PKG	Sweetener	Coconut palm sugar	35	4	g	4	0	1
G/USDA	Bakery	Cookie, Ranger Cookies, (From recipe in Are You Sweet Enough Already?)	35	80	g	9	10	3
B853	Dairy/Yoghurt	Yoghurt, red fruit: Morello cherry, Healthy Living Light, (UK)	35	200	g	12		4
B1270	Bread/Spec.	White bread 30 g, toasted, served with cheddar cheese 36 g, Hovis, (UK)	35	66	g	15		5
B1008	Fruit	Peach, dried (UK)	35	60	g	22		8
B1205	Con. Meal	Lamb moussaka, prepared convenience meal, Finest, (UK)	35	300	g	27		10
B895	Dairy/Yoghurt	Yoghurt, low fat, natural (UK)	35	200	g	35		12
B492	Grain	Barley, pearled, boiled 60 min (UK)	35	150	g	42		15
B862	Dairy/Yoghurt	Yoghurt, summer fruit: strawberry, Healthy Living Light, (UK)	36	200	g	13		5
B743	Snack	Crackers, Wholewheat with pumpkin and thyme (UK)UK)	36	25	g	15		6
B847	Dairy/Yoghurt	Yoghurt, Greek style, honey topped (UK)	36	200	g	32		12
B1151	Meal Repl. & Weight Mgmt.	SlimFast® Double Chocolate meal replacement powder, prepared with skim milk, SlimFast Foods Ltd, UK)	36	50	g	46		17
B854	Dairy/Yoghurt	Yoghurt, red fruit: raspberry and black cherry, Healthy Living Light, (UK)	37	200	g	13		5
B846	Dairy/Yoghurt	Yoghurt, Devonshire fudge, Finest, (UK)	37	200	g	34		13
B228	Bread/Spec.	White bread, prepared with a 10 min prove and a second 2 min proving low loaf volume) (UK)	38	30	g	13		5

GLYCEMIC INDEX (GI)

REF#	CATEGORY	FOOD	GI	SERV	UM	CARB	FIBRE	GL
B867	Dairy/Yoghurt	Yoghurt, tropical pineapple, Healthy Living Light, (UK)	38	200	g	13		5
G/USDA	Snack	Apple slices with peanut butter	38	120	g	23	5	9
G/USDA	Snack	Apple slices with peanut butter	38	120	g	23	5	9
B630	Digestive	Digestives (UK)	39	25	g	16		6
B1132	Meal Repl. & Weight Mgmt.	Chocolate weight management drink (UK)	39	250	mL	18		7
B1228	Vegetable/Spec.	Potato, Estima, 50 g, microwaved 6 min then baked 10 min, served with cheddar cheese 62 g (UK)	39	112	g	26		10
G/USDA	Snack	Dill Pickle	40	28	g	0.6	0.3	0
G/USDA	Vegetable	Radish	40	30	g	1	1	0
G/USDA	Vegetable	Watercress	40	120	g	2	1	1
G/USDA/#	Fruit	Strawberries	40	120	g	3	2	1
USDA/#	Pulses	Cocoa powder, unsweetened	40	5	g	3	1	1
G/USDA	Vegetable	Arugula	40	120	g	4	2	2
G/USDA	Vegetable	Celery	40	120	g	4	2	2
G/USDA	Vegetable	Swiss chard	40	120	g	4	2	2
G/USDA	Vegetable	Cucumber	40	120	g	4	1	2
G/USDA	Vegetable	Mushrooms	40	120	g	4	1	2
G/USDA	Vegetable	Zucchini	40	120	g	4	1	2
G/USDA	Vegetable	Asparagus	40	120	g	5	3	2
USDA/#	Pulses	Carob powder, unsweetened	40	6	g	5	2	2
G/USDA/#	Fruit	Rhubarb	40	120	g	5	2	2
G/USDA	Vegetable	Ginger root	40	28	g	5	1	2
G/USDA	Vegetable	Radiccio	40	120	g	5	1	2

GLYCEMIC INDEX (GI)

REF#	CATEGORY	FOOD	GI	SERV	UM	CARB	FIBRE	GL
G/USDA	Vegetable	Tomato	40	120	g	5	1	2
G/USDA	Vegetable	Collard greens	40	120	g	6	5	2
G/USDA	Vegetable	Cauliflower	40	120	g	6	2	2
G/USDA	Vegetable	Mustard greens	40	120	g	7	9	3
G/USDA	Vegetable	Eggplant	40	120	g	7	4	3
G/USDA	Vegetable	Kohlrabi	40	120	g	7	4	3
G/USDA/#	Vegetable	Olives	40	120	g	7	4	3
G/USDA	Snack	Celery with Hummus	40	80	g	7	3	0
G/USDA	Vegetable	Cabbage	40	120	g	7	3	3
G/USDA	Vegetable	Tomatillo	40	120	g	7	2	3
G/USDA	Vegetable	Bok Choy	40	120	g	7	1	3
G/USDA	Vegetable	Green Beans	40	120	g	8	4	3
G/USDA	Vegetable	Okra	40	120	g	8	4	3
G/USDA	Vegetable	Broccoli	40	120	g	8	3	3
G/USDA/#	Fruit	Figs	40	28	g	8	1	3
G/USDA	Vegetable	Garlic	40	28	g	8	1	3
G/USDA	Vegetable	Grape leaves	40	60	g	10	7	4
G/USDA	Snack	Celery with Cashew Butter	40	80	g	10	2	2
G/USDA/#	Fruit	Cantaloupe	40	120	g	10	1	4
G/USDA/#	Fruit	Rose hips	40	28	g	11	7	4
G/USDA	Vegetable	Jicama	40	120	g	11	6	4
G/USDA	Vegetable	Dandelion greens	40	120	g	11	4	4
G/USDA	Vegetable	Bell pepper	40	120	g	11	2	4

GLYCEMIC INDEX (GI)

REF#	CATEGORY	FOOD	GI	SERV	UM	CARB	FIBRE	GL
G/USDA	Vegetable	Kale	40	120	g	11	2	4
G/USDA	Vegetable	Onion	40	120	g	11	2	4
G/USDA/#	Fruit	Honeydew	40	120	g	11	1	4
G/USDA	Snack	Chocolado Parfait with a Cherry, (From recipe in Are You Sweet Enough Already?)	40	113	g	12	6	5
G/USDA	Vegetable	Beet greens	40	120	g	12	3	5
G/USDA/#	Fruit	Mulberries	40	120	g	12	2	5
G/USDA	Vegetable	Artichoke	40	120	g	13	6	5
G/USDA/#	Fruit	Apricot	40	120	g	13	2	5
G/USDA/#	Fruit	Papaya	40	120	g	13	2	5
G/USDA/#	Fruit	Plum	40	120	g	13	2	5
G/USDA/#	Fruit	Biosenberries	40	120	g	14	6	0
G/USDA/#	Fruit	Cranberries	40	120	g	14	6	6
G/USDA/#	Fruit	Cherries, red	40	120	g	14	2	6
G/USDA	Vegetable	Wheatgrass	40	30	g	16	8	6
G/USDA/#	Fruit	Pineapple	40	120	g	16	2	3
G/USDA/#	Fruit	Mandarin	40	120	g	16	2	7
G/USDA/#	Fruit	Tangerine	40	120	g	16	2	7
G/USDA/#	Fruit	Guava	40	120	g	17	6	7
G/USDA	Vegetable	Leek	40	120	g	17	2	7
G/USDA	Vegetable	Turmeric root	40	28	g	18	6	7
G/USDA/#	Fruit	Kiwi	40	120	g	18	4	6
G/USDA/#	Fruit	Mango	40	120	g	18	2	7
B699	Bakery	Cookie, Rich Tea (UK)	40	25	g	18		7

GLYCEMIC INDEX (GI)

REF#	CATEGORY	FOOD	GI	SERV	UM	CARB	FIBRE	GL
G/USDA	Bakery	Chocolate Black Bean Cake (From recipe in Are You Sweet Enough Already?)	40	80	g	19	4	8
G/USDA/#	Fruit	Soursop	40	120	g	20	4	2
G/USDA/#	Fruit	Lychee	40	120	g	20	2	4
B465	Cereal/Spec.	Porridge, jumbo oats (UK)Sainsbury's, UK), consumed with semi-skimmed milk	40	250	g	22		9
G/USDA/#	Fruit	Pomegranate	40	120	g	23	9	2
B455	Cereal/Spec.	Hot oat cereal, 30 g, cocoa flavor (UK) prepared with 125 mL skim milk	40	155	g	23		9
B460	Cereal/Spec.	Hot oat cereal, 30 g prepared with 125 mL skim milk (UK)	40	155	g	23		9
G/USDA/#	Fruit	Passionfruit	40	120	g	28	12	5
B1195	Con. Meal	Cumberland fish pie (UK)	40	300	g	31		12
G/USDA/#	Fruit	Plantain	40	120	g	38	3	10
G/USDA/#	Fruit	Persimmon	40	120	g	41	4	4
B1219	Pasta/Spec.	Fusilli pasta twists, Tesco Stores Ltd, UK), boiled 10 min in salted water, served with chilli con carne (UK)	40			48		19
B863	Dairy/Yoghurt	Yoghurt, toffee, Healthy Living Light, (UK)	41	200	g	16		7
B882	Dairy/Yoghurt	Yoghurt, Low-fat, black cherry (UK)	41	200	g	28		11
B858	Dairy/Yoghurt	Yoghurt, strawberry and cream, Finest, (UK)	41	200	g	38		16
B1257	Con. Meal	Sweet and sour chicken with noodles, prepared convenience meal, Serves One, (UK)	41	300	g	52		21
B473	Cereal	Breakfast Cereal bar, cranberry flavor (UK)	42	30	g	15		6
G/USDA	Fruit	Banana, slightly under-ripe, yellow with green	42	120	g	25	3	11

GLYCEMIC INDEX (GI)

REF#	CATEGORY	FOOD	GI	SERV	UM	CARB	FIBRE	GL
		sections						
B855	Dairy/Yoghurt	Yoghurt, red fruit: raspberry and cranberry, Healthy Living Light, (UK)	42	200	g	27		11
B881	Dairy/Yoghurt	Yoghurt, Low-fat, apricot (UK)	42	200	g	28		12
B849	Dairy/Yoghurt	Yoghurt, orange blossom, Finest, (UK)	42	200	g	40		17
B1200	Con. Meal	Fajitas, chicken (UK)	42	300	g	42		18
B1186	Con. Meal	Chilli beef noodles, prepared convenience meal, Finest, (UK)	42	300	g	46		19
B312	Cereal	Bran cereal, high fiber (UK)	43	30	g	12		5
B852	Dairy/Yoghurt	Yoghurt, raspberry, Healthy Living Light, (UK)	43	200	g	16		7
B1147	Meal Repl. & Weight Mgmt.	Malt toffee weight management bar (UK)	43	50	g	24		10
B454	Cereal/Spec.	Hot oat cereal 30 g, berry flavor (UK) prepared with 125 mL skim milk	43	155	g	26		11
B1012	Fruit	Pear, dried (UK)	43	60	g	27		12
B557	Grain	Rice, Basmati, white, boiled, Sainsbury's, (UK)	43	150	g	43		18
B908	Dairy/Yoghurt	Yoghurt, probiotic, prune (UK)	44	200	g	29		13
B1181	Con. Meal	Chicken korma and peshwari rice, prepared meal,Finest, UK)	44	300	g	48		21
B676	Bakery	Cookie, Oat biscuit (UK)	45	25	g	15		7
B909	Dairy/Yoghurt	Yoghurt, probiotic, raspberry (UK)	45	200	g	29		13
B1182	Con. Meal	Chicken korma and rice, convenience meal, Healthy Living, (UK)	45	300	g	48		21
B1258	Con. Meal	Tandoori chicken masala & rice convenience meal, Finest, (UK)	45	300	g	61		27
B789	Dairy	Milk, Full-fat, standardised homogenised, pasteurised, British Dairycrest, (UK)	46	250	mL	12		5
B1540	Soup	Chicken and mushroom	46	250	g	18		8

GLYCEMIC INDEX (GI)

REF#	CATEGORY	FOOD	GI	SERV	UM	CARB	FIBRE	GL
		soup (UK)						
B460.1	Cereal/Spec.	Cereal, Hot oat cereal mean of seven foods prepared with 125 mL skim milk	46	155	g	24		11
B469	Cereal/Spec.	Wheat Cereal biscuit 30 g, cocoa flavor, consumed with 125 mL skim milk (UK)	46	155	g	27		12
B1383	Pasta	Tagliatelle, egg pasta, boiled in water for 7 min (UK)	46	180	g	44		20
B869	Dairy/Yoghurt	Yoghurt, vanilla, Healthy Living Light, (UK)	47	200	g	14		7
B459	Cereal/Spec.	Hot oat cereal 30 g prepared with 125 mL skim milk	47	155	g	23		11
B456	Cereal/Spec.	Hot oat cereal, 30 g, fruit flavor (UK) prepared with 125 mL skim milk	47	155	g	25		12
B457	Cereal/Spec.	Hot oat cereal, 30 g, honey flavor (UK), prepared with 125 mL skim milk	47	155	g	26		12
B472	Cereal/Spec.	Wheat Cereal biscuit 30 g, wheat based, consumed with 125 mL skim milk (UK)	47	155	g	26		12
B910.1	Dairy/Yoghurt	Yoghurt, probiotic, mean of three foods	47	200	g	29		14
B1206	Con. Meal	Lasagne, beef, frozen (UK)	47	300	g	35		17
B1189	Con. Meal	Chow mein, chicken, convenience meal, Serves One, (UK)	47	300	g	38		18
B1599	Sweetener	Lactose, 25 g portion, DBH, Poole, (UK)	48	10	g	10		5
B818	Dairy	Milk, skimmed, pasteurised, British Dairycrest, (UK)	48	250	mL	13		6
B1253	Con. Meal	Steak and ale with cheddar mash potato convenience meal, Finest, (UK)	48	300	g	26		12
B278	Bread	Seeded bread (UK)	49	30	g	11		6
B716	Snack	Crackers, Choice grain (UK)	49	25	g	16		8
B464	Cereal/Spec.	Muesli, Wheat free, Pertwee Farm's, (UK),	49	30	g	19		9

GLYCEMIC INDEX (GI)

REF#	CATEGORY	FOOD	GI	SERV	UM	CARB	FIBRE	GL
		consumed with semi-skimmed milk						
B1499	Snack	Tropical fruit and nut mix, Finest, UK)	49	50	g	28		14
B1150	Meal Repl. & Weight Mgmt.	SlimFast® Chocolate Muesli snack bar, SlimFast Foods Ltd, UK)	49	50	g	32		16
B845	Dairy/Yoghurt	Yoghurt, champagne rhubarb, Finest, (UK)	49	200	g	38		19
B532	Grain	Rice, American, easy-cook rice, Sainsbury's, (UK)	49	150	g	46		22
B744	Snack	Crackers, Wholewheat sticks, crunchy, yeast extract flavored (UK)	50	25	g	14		7
B188	Bread	White wheat flour bread, toasted, Hovis, (UK)	50	41	g	15		7
B313	Cereal	Branflakes, Healthy Living, (UK)	50	30	g	20		10
B1269	Bread/Spec.	White bread 30 g, toasted, served with baked beans 51 g, Hovis, (UK)	50	81	g	21		11
B472.1	Cereal/Spec.	Wheat Cereal biscuit, consumed with 125 mL skim milk, mean of four foods	50	155	g	27		13
B1264	Bread/Spec.	White bread roll with cheese (UK)	50	100	g	40		20
B1111	Pulses	Red Kidney Beans, dried, soaked overnight, boiled 60 min (UK)	51	150	g	24		12
B1333	Pasta	Fusilli pasta twists, tricolour, dry pasta, boiled 10 min in unsalted water (UK)	51	180	g	45		23
B256	Bread	Crusty malted wheat bread, Finest, (UK)	52	30	g	13		7
B342	Cereal	High-fiber cereal (UK)	52	30	g	17		9
A744/USDA	South American	Corn tortilla (Mexican)	52	50	g	24	1	12
B471	Cereal/Spec.	Wheat Cereal biscuit 30 g, honey flavor, consumed with 125 mL skim milk (UK)	52	155	g	27		14
B558	Grain/Spec.	Rice, Basmati, white, boiled 12 min, Value, (UK)	52	150	g	28		15

GLYCEMIC INDEX (GI)

REF#	CATEGORY	FOOD	GI	SERV	UM	CARB	FIBRE	GL
B558	Grain/Spec.	Rice, Basmati, white, boiled 12 min, Value, (UK)	52	150	g	28		15
B910	Dairy/Yoghurt	Yoghurt, probiotic, strawberry (UK)	52	200	g	29		15
B524	Grain	Long grain, white, pre-cooked, microwaved 2 min, Express Rice, plain, Uncle Ben's, Masterfoods, (UK)	52	150	g	37		19
A280	Grain	Long grain white precooked microwaved 2 min, Express Rice plain Uncle Ben's; King's Lynn Norfolk (UK)	52	150	g	37		19
B1343	Pasta	Lasagne, egg, verdi, dry pasta, boiled in unsalted water for 10 min (UK)	52	180	g	45		23
B1173	Con. Meal	Beef and ale casserole, convenience meal Finest, (UK)	53	300	g	15		8
B742	Snack	Crackers, Wholegrain with sesame seeds and rosemary (UK)	53	25	g	16		8
B883	Dairy/Yoghurt	Yoghurt, Low-fat, hazelnut (UK)	53	200	g	29		15
B1154	Meal Repl. & Weight Mgmt.	SlimFast® Pasta Florentina meal, SlimFast Foods, UK)	53	250	g	34		12
B1342	Pasta	Lasagne, egg, dry pasta, boiled in unsalted water for 10 min(UK)	53	180	g	43		23
B1343.1	Pasta	Lasagne, egg, verdi, boiled in unsalted water for 10 min, mean of three studies	53	180	g	45		24
B273	Bread	Multiseed bread (UK)	54	30	g	12		7
B194	Bread/Spec.	White wheat flour bread, homemade, frozen, defrosted	54	30	g	13		7
B453	Cereal/Spec.	Honey Crunch cereal 30 g, consumed with 125 mL skim milk (UK)	54	155	g	30		16
B870	Dairy/Yoghurt	Yoghurt, white peach, Finest, (UK)	54	200	g	32		17
B1148	Meal Repl. & Weight Mgmt.	SlimFast® chocolate caramel meal replacement bar, SlimFast Foods Ltd,	54	50	g	33		18

GLYCEMIC INDEX (GI)

REF#	CATEGORY	FOOD	GI	SERV	UM	CARB	FIBRE	GL
		Slough, Berks, UK)						
B1335	Pasta	Gluten-free pasta, maize starch, boiled 8 min (UK)	54	180	g	42		23
A522	Pasta	Gluten-free pasta maize starch boiled 8 min (UK)	54	180	g	42		22
B1384	Pasta	Tagliatelle, egg, boiled, Sainsbury's, UK)	54	180	g	44		24
B1332	Pasta	Fusilli pasta twists, dry pasta, boiled in 10 min in unsalted water (UK)	54	180	g	48		26
H/USDA	Snack	Microwave popcorn plain, average	55	20	g	11	3	6
PKG	Sweetener	Blackstrap molasses	55	15	mL	13	0	7
B355	Cereal	Muesli, Alpen original, made from steamed rolled oats with dried fruit and nuts, Weetabix, (UK)	55	30	g	19		11
B1188	Con. Meal	Chow mein, chicken, convenience meal, Healthy Living, (UK)	55	300	g	23		13
B1334	Pasta	Fusilli pasta twists, wholewheat, dry pasta, boiled 10 min in unsalted water (UK)	55	180	g	41		23
B1334.1	Pasta	Fusilli pasta, twists, mean of four studies	55	180	g	46		25
B1341	Pasta	Lasagne sheets, dry pasta, boiled in unsalted water for 10 min, Value, UK)	55	180	g	47		26
B1066	Infant Foods	Apple, apricot and banana cereal, Robinsons first Tastes from 4 months, Nutricia, Wells, (UK)	56	75	g	13		7
A447.1	Infant foods	Apple apricot and banana cereal6, Robinsons First Tastes from 4 months, Nutricia Wells, (UK)	56	75	g	13		11
B296	Bread	Pita bread, unleavened, wholemeal (UK)	56	30	g	14		8
B376	Cereal	Muesli, wholewheat (UK)	56	30	g	18		10

GLYCEMIC INDEX (GI)

REF#	CATEGORY	FOOD	GI	SERV	UM	CARB	FIBRE	GL
B470	Cereal/Spec.	Wheat Cereal biscuit 30 g, fruit flavor, consumed with 125 mL skim milk (UK)	56	155	g	27		15
B884	Dairy/Yoghurt	Yoghurt, Low-fat, peach melba, Value, (UK)	56	200	g	28		16
B1048	Beverage	Cranberry juice drink, Ocean Spray®, Gerber Ltd., Bridgewater, Somerset, (UK)	56	250	mL	29		16
A39	Beverage	Cranberry juice drink Ocean Spray, Gerber Ltd Bridgewater (UK)	56	250	mL	29		16
A402	Beverage	Cranberry juice drink, Ocean Spray; Gerber Ltd Bridgewater Somerset(UK)	56	250	mL	29		16
B919	Dairy/Yoghurt	Yoghurt, Probiotic drink, cranberry (UK)	56	250	mL	31		17
B1640	Vegetable	Potato, Marfona, peeled, quartered, boiled 15 min in unsalted water (UK)UK)	56	150	g	32		18
B1030	Fruit	Sultanas, Value, (UK)	56	60	g	42		23
B137	Bread	Fruit loaf, sliced (UK)	57	30	g	16		9
B734	Snack	Crackers, Rye with sesame (UK)	57	25	g	16		9
B450	Cereal/Spec.	Cereal flakes with fruit (UK)30 g), consumed with 125 mL skim milk (UK)UK)	57	155	g	29		16
B851	Dairy/Yoghurt	Yoghurt, peach melba, Value, (UK)	57	200	g	32		18
B559	Grain/Spec.	Rice, Basmati, white, organic, boiled 10 min (UK)	57	150	g	40		23
B565	Grain	Rice, Precooked basmati rice in pouch, white, reheated in microwave, Uncle Ben's Express® Masterfoods, (UK)	57	150	g	41		24
A297	Grain	Precooked basmati rice in pouch white reheated in microwave, Uncle Ben's Express; Masterfoods. Kings Lynn Norfolk (UK)	57	150	g	41		24
A318	Digestive	Digestives gluten-free, maize starch, Nutricia	58	25	g	17		10

GLYCEMIC INDEX (GI)

REF#	CATEGORY	FOOD	GI	SERV	UM	CARB	FIBRE	GL
		Dietary Care Ltd Redish Stockport (UK)						
B451	Cereal/Spec.	Cocoa Crunch cereal 30 g with 125 mL skim milk (UK)	58	155	g	28		16
B1031	Fruit	Sultanas (UK)	58	60	g	42		24
B1067	Infant Foods	Creamed rice porridge, Robinsons first Tastes from 4 months, Nutricia, Wells, (UK)	59	75	g	9		5
A447.2	Infant foods	Creamed porridge, Robinsons First Tastes from 4 months, Nutricia Wells (UK)	59	75	g	9		5
B1068	Infant Foods	Rice pudding, Robinsons first Tastes from 4 months, Nutricia, Wells, (UK)	59	75	g	11		6
A447.3	Infant foods	Rice pudding, Robinsons First Tastes from 4 months (Nutricia Wells UK)	59	75	g	11		6
B200	Bread/Spec.	White wheat flour bread with added wheatgerm and fiber with oat fiber (UK) (Italy)	59	30	g	12		6
B172	Bread	White flour (UK)	59	30	g	13		8
A356	Bread	Rye crispbread, High-fiber rye crispbread Ryvita Company Ltd Poole Dorset (UK)	59	25	g	15		9
B1642	Vegetable	Potato, Nicola, peeled, quartered, boiled 15 min (UK)	59	150	g	16		9
B363	Cereal	Muesli, fruit and nut (UK)	59	30	g	18		11
B265	Bread	Malt loaf, organic (UK)	59	30	g	21		12
B353	Cereal	Mini Wheats, whole wheat, Sainsbury's, (UK)	59	30	g	21		12
B467	Cereal/Spec.	Precise, Sainsbury's, (UK), with semi-skimmed milk	59	30	g	24		14
B190.1	Bread	White wheat flour bread, toasted, mean of three studies	60	30	g	13		8
B1557	Soup	Vegetable soup (UK)	60	250	g	18		11
B462	Cereal/Spec.	Muesli, Original, Sainsbury's, (UK), consumed with semi-	60	30	g	19		11

GLYCEMIC INDEX (GI)

REF#	CATEGORY	FOOD	GI	SERV	UM	CARB	FIBRE	GL
		skimmed milk						
B463	Cereal/Spec.	Muesli, Swiss, Sainsbury's, (UK), consumed with semi-skimmed milk	60	30	g	19		12
B992	Fruit	Mixed fruit, dried, Value, (UK)	60	60	g	41		24
B332	Cereal	Fruit and Fibre™, Sainsbury's, UK)	61	30	g	21		13
B466	Cereal/Spec.	Porridge, small oats, Sainsbury's, (UK), consumed with semi-skimmed milk	61	250	g	22		14
B886	Dairy/Yoghurt	Yoghurt, Low-fat, strawberry (UK)	61	200	g	30		18
B1249	Con. Meal	Sausages and mash potato, prepared convenience meal (UK)	61	300	g	40		25
B1331	Pasta	Fusilli pasta twists, Tesco Stores Ltd, UK), boiled 10 min in salted water (UK)	61	180	g	48		29
B192	Bread/Spec.	White wheat flour bread, homemade, frozen and defrosted (UK)	62	30	g	13		8
B268	Bread	Multigrain batch bread (UK)	62	30	g	14		9
B149	Bread	Oatmeal batch bread (UK)	62	30	g	15		9
B1226	Vegetable/Spec.	Potato, Estima, 50 g, microwaved 6 min then baked 10 min, served with baked beans, 89 g, (UK)	62	139	g	37		23
B189	Bread	White wheat flour bread, fresh, toasted British Bakeries Ltd, (UK)	63	40	g	12		8
A356	Bread	Rye crispbread Ryvita Company Ltd (UK)	63	25	g	18		11
B397	Cereal	Porridge, organic, made from rolled oats (UK)	63	250	g	29		18
B396	Cereal	Porridge made from rolled oats, Value, UK)	63	250	g	30		19
B398	Cereal	Porridge, made from rolled oats, Scottish (UK)	63	250	g	31		20
B193	Bread/Spec.	White wheat flour bread, frozen, defrosted and toasted, British Bakeries	64	30	g	12		8

GLYCEMIC INDEX (GI)

REF#	CATEGORY	FOOD	GI	SERV	UM	CARB	FIBRE	GL
		Ltd, (UK)						
B733	Snack	Crackers, Rye with oats (UK)	64	25	g	16		10
B359	Cereal	Muesli, Value, UK)	64	30	g	19		12
B844	Dairy/Yoghurt	Yoghurt, bourbon vanilla, Finest, (UK)	64	200	g	32		20
B334.1	Cereal	Fruit and Fibre, mean of three studies	65	30	g	21		13
B452	Cereal/Spec.	Cornflakes, Sainsbury's, (UK) 30 g, consumed with 125 mL skim milk	65	30	g	25		16
B1194	Con. Meal	Cottage pie (UK)	65	300	g	34		22
B245	Bread	Wholemeal flour, stoneground whole wheat, Waitrose,(UK)	66	30	g	12		8
B190	Bread	White wheat flour bread, homemade, fresh, toasted (UK)	66	40	g	13		9
B1634	Vegetable	Potato, Charlotte, peeled, quartered, boiled 15 min (UK)	66	150	g	23		15
B1637	Vegetable	Potato, Estima, peeled, quartered, boiled 15 min (UK)	66	150	g	26		17
B1251	Con. Meal	Shepherds pie, prepared convenience meal (UK)	66	300	g	44		29
B843	Dairy/Yoghurt	Yoghurt, black cherry, Healthy Living Light, (UK)	67	200	g	12		8
B333	Cereal	Fruit and Fibre (UK)	67	30	g	21		14
B362	Cereal	Muesli, fruit (UK)	67	30	g	21		14
B563	Grain/Spec.	Rice, Basmati, easy cook, white, boiled 9 min (UK)	67	150	g	42		28
B848	Dairy/Yoghurt	Yoghurt, lemon curd, Finest, (UK)	67	200	g	45		30
B234	Bread	Wholemeal whole wheat, wheat flour bread Hovis, (UK)	68	30	g	11		7
B295	Bread	Pita bread, unleavened, white, mini (UK)	68	30	g	15		10
B334	Cereal	Fruit and Fibre, Value, (UK)	68	30	g	20		13
B564	Grain	Rice, Basmati, easy-cook rice, boiled, Sainsbury's, (UK)	68	150	g	41		28

GLYCEMIC INDEX (GI)

REF#	CATEGORY	FOOD	GI	SERV	UM	CARB	FIBRE	GL
A78.1	Bread	Gluten-free fiber-enriched bread, unsliced gluten-free wheat starch soya bran) (UK)	69	30	g	13		9
B1541	Soup	Chicken and mushroom soup (UK)	69	250	g	19		13
B1627	Vegetable	Potato, white, baked with skin, baked (UK)	69	150	g	27		19
B562	Grain/Spec.	Rice, Basmati, white, boiled 8 min (UK)	69	150	g	40		28
B111	Bread	Barley, Sunflower and barley bread Vogel's, (UK), course 80% kernels	70	30	g	12		8
B175	Bread	White wheat flour bread, Sainsbury's, (UK)	70	30	g	14		10
B236	Bread	Wholemeal whole wheat, wheat flour bread Sainsbury's,(UK)	71	30	g	11		8
A77.1	Bread	Gluten-free white bread gluten-free wheat starch (UK), Unsliced	71	30	g	15		11
B135	Bread	Fruit and cinnamon bread, Finest, (UK)	71	30	g	16		11
B229	Bread/Spec.	White bread, prepared with a 30 min prove and a second 12 min proving moderate loaf volume (UK)	72	30	g	13		9
B441	Cereal	Wheat based cereal biscuit (UK) (Plain flaked wheat)	72	30	g	20		14
A78.3	Bread	Gluten-free fiber-enriched bread, Mean of 2 studies	73	30	g	13		9
B180	Bread	White wheat flour bread, Hovis, (UK)	73	30	g	15		11
B239	Bread	Wholemeal whole wheat, wheat flour bread Hovis, (UK)	74	30	g	11		8
A142	Bread	Whole-wheat snack bread, Ryvita Co Ltd Poole Dorset (UK)	74	30	g	22		16
B304	Cereal	Balance™, Sainsbury's, (UK)	74	30	g	23		17
B191	Bread/Spec.	White wheat flour bread, frozen and defrosted British Bakeries Ltd, (UK)	75	30	g	12		9

GLYCEMIC INDEX (GI)

REF#	CATEGORY	FOOD	GI	SERV	UM	CARB	FIBRE	GL
B183	Bread	White wheat flour bread, Hovis, (UK)	75	30	g	15		11
B1639	Vegetable	Potato, King Edward potato, peeled, quartered, boiled 15 min in unsalted water (UK)	75	150	g	28		21
B1229	Vegetable/Spec.	Potato, Estima 50 g, microwaved 6 min then baked 10 min, served with chilli con carne, 63 g (UK)	75	113	g	31		23
A78.2	Bread	Gluten-free fiber-enriched bread, sliced gluten-free wheat starch soya bran (UK)	76	30	g	13		10
A77.3	Bread	Gluten-free white bread gluten-free wheat starch (UK), Mean of 2 studies	76	30	g	15		11
B449	Cereal/Spec.	Branflakes, Sainsbury's, (UK), with semi-skimmed milk	76	30	g	20		15
B1227	Vegetable/Spec.	Potato, Estima, 50 g, microwaved 6 min then baked 10 min, served with canned tuna, 62 g (UK)	76	112	g	26		20
B267	Bread	Multigrain bread, Sainsbury's, (UK)	80	30	g	10		8
A77.2	Bread	Gluten-free white bread gluten-free wheat starch) (UK), Sliced	80	30	g	15		12
B1680	Vegetable	Potato, New, boiled (UK)	80	150	g	23		18
B468	Cereal/Spec.	Rice Pops™, Sainsbury's, (UK), with semi-skimmed milk	80	30	g	25		20
B1635	Vegetable	Potato, Charlotte, boiled (UK)	81	150	g	23		19
B411	Cereal	Porridge, Instant oat cereal porridge prepared with water (UK)	83	250	g	36		30
B1641	Vegetable	Potato, Maris Piper, peeled, quartered, boiled 15 min in unsalted water (UK)	85	150	g	29		25
B230	Bread/Spec.	White bread, prepared with a 60 min prove and a second 30 min proving moderate loaf volume (UK)	86	30	g	13		11

GLYCEMIC INDEX (GI)

REF#	CATEGORY	FOOD	GI	SERV	UM	CARB	FIBRE	GL
B361	Cereal	Muesli, Healthy Eating, (UK)	86	30	g	21		18
B184	Bread	White wheat flour flour bread Hovis Classic, British Bakeries Ltd, (UK)	87	30	g	12		11
B187	Bread	White wheat flour bread, homemade (UK)	89	30	g	13		12
B325	Cereal	Cornflakes, Kellogg's, (UK)	93	30	g	25		23
B1674	Vegetable	Potato, Estima, microwaved 6 min then baked 10 min (UK)	93	150	g	26		24
A24	Beverage	Lucozade original, sparkling glucose drink) Glaxo Wellcome Ltd Uxbridge UK)	95	250	mL	42		40
B1651	Vegetable	Potato, white, boiled (UK)	96	150	g	26		24
B1630	Vegetable	Potato, white, baked without skin, baked (UK)	98	150	g	27		26
B231	Bread/Spec.	White bread, prepared with a 40 min prove, a second 25 min proving and a third 50 min proving large loaf volume (UK)	100	30	g	13		13
B1672	Vegetable	Potato, Desiree, mashed (UK)	102	150	g	26		26

GLYCEMIC INDEX (GI)

FIBRE

REF#	CATEGORY	FOOD	GI	SERV	UM	CARB	FIBRE	GL
USDA/#	Fruit	Passionfruit	40	120	g	28	12	5
G/USDA	Bakery	Cookie, Ranger Cookies, (From recipe in Are You Sweet Enough Already?)	35	80	g	9	10	3
G/USDA/#	Fruit	Pomegranate	40	120	g	23	9	2
G/USDA	Vegetable	Mustard greens	40	120	g	7	9	3
G/USDA	Fruit	Avocado	0	120	g	11	8	0
G/USDA	Fruit	Raspberries	0	120	g	15	8	3
G/USDA	Vegetable	Wheatgrass	40	30	g	16	8	6
G/USDA/#	Fruit	Rose hips	40	28	g	11	7	4
G/USDA	Vegetable	Grape leaves	40	60	g	10	7	4
G/USDA/#	Fruit	Boysenberries	40	120	g	14	6	0
G/USDA/#	Fruit	Cranberries	40	120	g	14	6	6
G/USDA/#	Fruit	Guava	40	120	g	17	6	7
G/USDA	Nuts	Almond meal flour	0	50	g	11	6	0
G/USDA	Nuts	Almonds	0	50	g	11	6	0
G/USDA	Snack	Chocolado Parfait with a Cherry, (From recipe in Are You Sweet Enough Already?)	40	113	g	12	6	5
G/USDA	Vegetable	Jicama	40	120	g	11	6	4
G/USDA	Vegetable	Artichoke	40	120	g	13	6	5
G/USDA	Vegetable	Turmeric root	40	28	g	18	6	7
G/USDA	Pulses	Chickpea (Garbanzo Bean) flour	10	30	g	18	5	2
G/USDA	Nuts	Pecans	0	50	g	7	5	0

FIBRE

REF#	CATEGORY	FOOD	GI	SERV	UM	CARB	FIBRE	GL
G/USDA	Nuts	Hazelnuts	0	50	g	8	5	0
G/USDA	Snack	Apple slices with peanut butter	38	120	g	23	5	9
G/USDA	Snack	Apple slices with peanut butter	38	120	g	23	5	9
A749/USDA	South American	Wheat tortilla (Mexican)	30	50	g	26	5	8
G/USDA	Vegetable	Collard greens	40	120	g	6	5	2
G/USDA	Bakery	Chocolate Black Bean Cake (From recipe in Are You Sweet Enough Already?)	40	80	g	19	4	8
G/USDA/#	Fruit	Blackberries	0	120	g	12	4	0
G/USDA/#	Fruit	Kiwi	40	120	g	18	4	6
G/USDA/#	Fruit	Soursop	40	120	g	20	4	2
G/USDA/#	Fruit	Persimmon	40	120	g	41	4	4
G/USDA	Nuts	Macadamia	0	50	g	7	4	0
G/USDA	Nuts	Walnuts	0	50	g	7	4	0
G/USDA	Vegetable	Eggplant	40	120	g	7	4	3
G/USDA	Vegetable	Kohlrabi	40	120	g	7	4	3
G/USDA/#	Vegetable	Olives	40	120	g	7	4	3
G/USDA	Vegetable	Green Beans	40	120	g	8	4	3
G/USDA	Vegetable	Okra	40	120	g	8	4	3
G/USDA	Vegetable	Dandelion greens	40	120	g	11	4	4
G/USDA	Fruit	Blueberries	29	120	g	17	3	5
G/USDA/#	Fruit	Plantain	40	120	g	38	3	10
G/USDA	Fruit	Banana, slightly under-ripe, yellow with green sections	42	120	g	25	3	11

FIBRE

REF#	CATEGORY	FOOD	GI	SERV	UM	CARB	FIBRE	GL
G/USDA	Snack	Celery with Hummus	40	80	g	7	3	0
H/USDA	Snack	Microwave popcorn plain, average	55	20	g	11	3	6
G/USDA	Vegetable	Spinach	0	150	g	4	3	0
G/USDA	Vegetable	Asparagus	40	120	g	5	3	2
G/USDA	Vegetable	Cabbage	40	120	g	7	3	3
G/USDA	Vegetable	Broccoli	40	120	g	8	3	3
G/USDA	Vegetable	Beet greens	40	120	g	12	3	5
USDA/#	Pulses	Carob powder, unsweetened	40	6	g	5	2	2
G/USDA/#	Fruit	Strawberries	40	120	g	3	2	1
G/USDA/#	Fruit	Rhubarb	40	120	g	5	2	2
G/USDA/#	Fruit	Mulberries	40	120	g	12	2	5
G/USDA/#	Fruit	Apricot	40	120	g	13	2	5
G/USDA/#	Fruit	Papaya	40	120	g	13	2	5
G/USDA/#	Fruit	Plum	40	120	g	13	2	5
G/USDA/#	Fruit	Cherries, red	40	120	g	14	2	6
G/USDA/#	Fruit	Pineapple	40	120	g	16	2	3
G/USDA/#	Fruit	Mandarin	40	120	g	16	2	7
G/USDA/#	Fruit	Tangerine	40	120	g	16	2	7
G/USDA/#	Fruit	Mango	40	120	g	18	2	7
G/USDA/#	Fruit	Lychee	40	120	g	20	2	4
H/USDA	Snack	Hummus, chickpea salad dip, commercially prepared	6	30	g	4	2	0
G/USDA	Snack	Celery with Cashew Butter	40	80	g	10	2	2
G/USDA	Vegetable	Green Leaf Lettuce	0	150	g	4	2	0

FIBRE

REF#	CATEGORY	FOOD	GI	SERV	UM	CARB	FIBRE	GL
G/USDA	Vegetable	Arugula	40	120	g	4	2	2
G/USDA	Vegetable	Celery	40	120	g	4	2	2
G/USDA	Vegetable	Swiss chard	40	120	g	4	2	2
G/USDA	Vegetable	Cauliflower	40	120	g	6	2	2
G/USDA	Vegetable	Tomatillo	40	120	g	7	2	3
G/USDA	Vegetable	Bell pepper	40	120	g	11	2	4
G/USDA	Vegetable	Kale	40	120	g	11	2	4
G/USDA	Vegetable	Onion	40	120	g	11	2	4
G/USDA	Vegetable	Leek	40	120	g	17	2	7
USDA/#	Pulses	Cocoa powder, unsweetened	40	5	g	3	1	1
G/USDA	Beverage	Almond Milk, unsweetened	0	226	mL	1	1	0
G/USDA/#	Fruit	Figs	40	28	g	8	1	3
G/USDA/#	Fruit	Cantaloupe	40	120	g	10	1	4
G/USDA/#	Fruit	Honeydew	40	120	g	11	1	4
A744/USDA	South American	Corn tortilla (Mexican)	52	50	g	24	1	12
G/USDA	Vegetable	Radish	40	30	g	1	1	0
G/USDA	Vegetable	Watercress	40	120	g	2	1	1
G/USDA	Vegetable	Cucumber	40	120	g	4	1	2
G/USDA	Vegetable	Mushrooms	40	120	g	4	1	2
G/USDA	Vegetable	Zucchini	40	120	g	4	1	2
G/USDA	Vegetable	Ginger root	40	28	g	5	1	2
G/USDA	Vegetable	Radiccio	40	120	g	5	1	2
G/USDA	Vegetable	Tomato	40	120	g	5	1	2

FIBRE

REF#	CATEGORY	FOOD	GI	SERV	UM	CARB	FIBRE	GL
G/USDA	Vegetable	Bok Choy	40	120	g	7	1	3
G/USDA	Vegetable	Garlic	40	28	g	8	1	3
G/USDA	Snack	Dill Pickle	40	28	g	0.6	0.3	0
USDA	Beverage	Coffee or tea, black, unsweetened	0			0	0	0
USDA	Beverage	Seltzer water, baking extract flavored, stevia sweetened	0			0	0	0
USDA	Beverage	Water	0			0	0	0
G/PKG	Beverage	Coconut Milk, unsweetened	0	240	mL	1	0	0
G/USDA	Dairy	Creamed cottage cheese	30	226	g	4	0	1
G/USDA	Meat, Fish & Poultry	All meat, fish, shellfish, poultry, including wild game or meats	0			0	0	0
G/USDA	Snack	Sardines, fish snacks, canned	0	95	g	0	0	0
G/USDA	Snack	Egg, hardboiled	0		g	1	0	0
PKG	Sweetener	Stevia extract	0			0	0	0
PKG	Sweetener	Stevia extract	0			0	0	0
PKG	Sweetener	Stevia	0	1	g	<1	0	0
PKG	Sweetener	Xylitol (1 packet)	7	2.04	g	2	0	0
PKG	Sweetener	Coconut palm sugar	35	4	g	4	0	1
PKG	Sweetener	Coconut palm sugar	35	4	g	4	0	1
PKG	Sweetener	Blackstrap molasses	55	15	mL	13	0	7
B699	Bakery	Cookie, Rich Tea (UK)	40	25	g	18		7
B676	Bakery	Cookie, Oat biscuit (UK)	45	25	g	15		7
B1115	Pulses	Lentils, red, split, dried, boiled 25 min (UK)	21	150	g	18		4
B1128	Pulses	Split peas, yellow, dried, soaked overnight, boiled 55 min (UK)	25	150	g	13		3
B1090	Pulses	Butter Beans, dried, soaked overnight, boiled 50 min (UK)	26	150	g	20		5
B1111	Pulses	Red Kidney Beans, dried, soaked overnight, boiled 60 min (UK)	51	150	g	24		12
G	Beverage	Beer, wine, spirits (no GI, but can have carbs, depending on brand)	0			0		

FIBRE

REF#	CATEGORY	FOOD	GI	SERV	UM	CARB	FIBRE	GL
B1048	Beverage	Cranberry juice drink, Ocean Spray®, Gerber Ltd., Bridgewater, Somerset, (UK)	56	250	mL	29		16
A39	Beverage	Cranberry juice drink Ocean Spray, Gerber Ltd Bridgewater (UK)	56	250	mL	29		16
A402	Beverage	Cranberry juice drink, Ocean Spray; Gerber Ltd Bridgewater Somerset(UK)	56	250	mL	29		16
A24	Beverage	Lucozade original, sparkling glucose drink) Glaxo Wellcome Ltd Uxbridge UK)	95	250	mL	42		40
B278	Bread	Seeded bread (UK)	49	30	g	11		6
B188	Bread	White wheat flour bread, toasted, Hovis, (UK)	50	41	g	15		7
B256	Bread	Crusty malted wheat bread, Finest, (UK)	52	30	g	13		7
B273	Bread	Multiseed bread (UK)	54	30	g	12		7
B296	Bread	Pita bread, unleavened, wholemeal (UK)	56	30	g	14		8
B137	Bread	Fruit loaf, sliced (UK)	57	30	g	16		9
B172	Bread	White flour (UK)	59	30	g	13		8
A356	Bread	Rye crispbread, High-fiber rye crispbread Ryvita Company Ltd Poole Dorset (UK)	59	25	g	15		9
B265	Bread	Malt loaf, organic (UK)	59	30	g	21		12
B190.1	Bread	White wheat flour bread, toasted, mean of three studies	60	30	g	13		8
B268	Bread	Multigrain batch bread (UK)	62	30	g	14		9
B149	Bread	Oatmeal batch bread (UK)	62	30	g	15		9
B189	Bread	White wheat flour bread, fresh, toasted British Bakeries Ltd, (UK)	63	40	g	12		8
A356	Bread	Rye crispbread Ryvita Company Ltd (UK)	63	25	g	18		11
B245	Bread	Wholemeal flour, stoneground whole wheat, Waitrose,(UK)	66	30	g	12		8
B190	Bread	White wheat flour bread, homemade, fresh, toasted (UK)	66	40	g	13		9

FIBRE

REF#	CATEGORY	FOOD	GI	SERV	UM	CARB	FIBRE	GL
B234	Bread	Wholemeal whole wheat, wheat flour bread Hovis, (UK)	68	30	g	11		7
B295	Bread	Pita bread, unleavened, white, mini (UK)	68	30	g	15		10
A78.1	Bread	Gluten-free fiber-enriched bread, unsliced gluten-free wheat starch soya bran) (UK)	69	30	g	13		9
B111	Bread	Barley, Sunflower and barley bread Vogel's, (UK), course 80% kernels	70	30	g	12		8
B175	Bread	White wheat flour bread, Sainsbury's, (UK)	70	30	g	14		10
B236	Bread	Wholemeal whole wheat, wheat flour bread Sainsbury's,(UK)	71	30	g	11		8
A77.1	Bread	Gluten-free white bread gluten-free wheat starch (UK), Unsliced	71	30	g	15		11
B135	Bread	Fruit and cinnamon bread, Finest, (UK)	71	30	g	16		11
A78.3	Bread	Gluten-free fiber-enriched bread, Mean of 2 studies	73	30	g	13		9
B180	Bread	White wheat flour bread, Hovis, (UK)	73	30	g	15		11
B239	Bread	Wholemeal whole wheat, wheat flour bread Hovis, (UK)	74	30	g	11		8
A142	Bread	Whole-wheat snack bread, Ryvita Co Ltd Poole Dorset (UK)	74	30	g	22		16
B183	Bread	White wheat flour bread, Hovis, (UK)	75	30	g	15		11
A78.2	Bread	Gluten-free fiber-enriched bread, sliced gluten-free wheat starch soya bran (UK)	76	30	g	13		10
A77.3	Bread	Gluten-free white bread gluten-free wheat starch (UK), Mean of 2 studies	76	30	g	15		11
B267	Bread	Multigrain bread, Sainsbury's, (UK)	80	30	g	10		8
A77.2	Bread	Gluten-free white bread gluten-free wheat starch) (UK), Sliced	80	30	g	15		12

FIBRE

REF#	CATEGORY	FOOD	GI	SERV	UM	CARB	FIBRE	GL
B184	Bread	White wheat flour flour bread Hovis Classic, British Bakeries Ltd, (UK)	87	30	g	12		11
B187	Bread	White wheat flour bread, homemade (UK)	89	30	g	13		12
B1270	Bread/Spec.	White bread 30 g, toasted, served with cheddar cheese 36 g, Hovis, (UK)	35	66	g	15		5
B228	Bread/Spec.	White bread, prepared with a 10 min prove and a second 2 min proving low loaf volume) (UK)	38	30	g	13		5
B1269	Bread/Spec.	White bread 30 g, toasted, served with baked beans 51 g, Hovis, (UK)	50	81	g	21		11
B1264	Bread/Spec.	White bread roll with cheese (UK)	50	100	g	40		20
B194	Bread/Spec.	White wheat flour bread, homemade, frozen, defrosted	54	30	g	13		7
B200	Bread/Spec.	White wheat flour bread with added wheatgerm and fiber with oat fiber (UK) (Italy)	59	30	g	12		6
B193	Bread/Spec.	White wheat flour bread, frozen, defrosted and toasted, British Bakeries Ltd, (UK)	64	30	g	12		8
B229	Bread/Spec.	White bread, prepared with a 30 min prove and a second 12 min proving moderate loaf volume (UK)	72	30	g	13		9
B191	Bread/Spec.	White wheat flour bread, frozen and defrosted British Bakeries Ltd, (UK)	75	30	g	12		9
B230	Bread/Spec.	White bread, prepared with a 60 min prove and a second 30 min proving moderate loaf volume (UK)	86	30	g	13		11
B231	Bread/Spec.	White bread, prepared with a 40 min prove, a second 25 min proving and a third 50 min proving large loaf volume	100	30	g	13		13

FIBRE

REF#	CATEGORY	FOOD	GI	SERV	UM	CARB	FIBRE	GL
		(UK)						
B192	Bread/Spec.	White wheat flour bread, homemade, frozen and defrosted (UK)	62	30	g	13		8
B474	Cereal	Breakfast Cereal bar, hazelnut flavor (UK)	33	30	g	11		4
B475	Cereal	Breakfast Cereal bar, orange flavor (UK)	33	30	g	14		5
B473	Cereal	Breakfast Cereal bar, cranberry flavor (UK)	42	30	g	15		6
B312	Cereal	Bran cereal, high fiber (UK)	43	30	g	12		5
B313	Cereal	Branflakes, Healthy Living, (UK)	50	30	g	20		10
B342	Cereal	High-fiber cereal (UK)	52	30	g	17		9
B355	Cereal	Muesli, Alpen original, made from steamed rolled oats with dried fruit and nuts, Weetabix, (UK)	55	30	g	19		11
B376	Cereal	Muesli, wholewheat (UK)	56	30	g	18		10
B363	Cereal	Muesli, fruit and nut (UK)	59	30	g	18		11
B353	Cereal	Mini Wheats, whole wheat, Sainsbury's, (UK)	59	30	g	21		12
B332	Cereal	Fruit and Fibre™, Sainsbury's, UK)	61	30	g	21		13
B397	Cereal	Porridge, organic, made from rolled oats (UK)	63	250	g	29		18
B396	Cereal	Porridge made from rolled oats, Value, UK)	63	250	g	30		19
B398	Cereal	Porridge, made from rolled oats, Scottish (UK)	63	250	g	31		20
B359	Cereal	Muesli, Value, UK)	64	30	g	19		12
B334.1	Cereal	Fruit and Fibre, mean of three studies	65	30	g	21		13
B333	Cereal	Fruit and Fibre (UK)	67	30	g	21		14
B362	Cereal	Muesli, fruit (UK)	67	30	g	21		14
B334	Cereal	Fruit and Fibre, Value, (UK)	68	30	g	20		13
B441	Cereal	Wheat based cereal biscuit (UK) (Plain flaked wheat)	72	30	g	20		14
B304	Cereal	Balance™, Sainsbury's, (UK)	74	30	g	23		17

FIBRE

REF#	CATEGORY	FOOD	GI	SERV	UM	CARB	FIBRE	GL
B411	Cereal	Porridge, Instant oat cereal porridge prepared with water (UK)	83	250	g	36		30
B361	Cereal	Muesli, Healthy Eating, (UK)	86	30	g	21		18
B325	Cereal	Cornflakes, Kellogg's, (UK)	93	30	g	25		23
B458	Cereal/Spec.	Hot oat cereal 30 g, orchard fruit flavor (UK) prepared with 125 mL skim milk	5	155	g	25		12
B465	Cereal/Spec.	Porridge, jumbo oats (UK)Sainsbury's, UK), consumed with semi-skimmed milk	40	250	g	22		9
B455	Cereal/Spec.	Hot oat cereal, 30 g, cocoa flavor (UK) prepared with 125 mL skim milk	40	155	g	23		9
B460	Cereal/Spec.	Hot oat cereal, 30 g prepared with 125 mL skim milk (UK)	40	155	g	23		9
B454	Cereal/Spec.	Hot oat cereal 30 g, berry flavor (UK) prepared with 125 mL skim milk	43	155	g	26		11
B460.1	Cereal/Spec.	Cereal, Hot oat cereal mean of seven foods prepared with 125 mL skim milk	46	155	g	24		11
B469	Cereal/Spec.	Wheat Cereal biscuit 30 g, cocoa flavor, consumed with 125 mL skim milk (UK)	46	155	g	27		12
B459	Cereal/Spec.	Hot oat cereal 30 g prepared with 125 mL skim milk	47	155	g	23		11
B456	Cereal/Spec.	Hot oat cereal, 30 g, fruit flavor (UK) prepared with 125 mL skim milk	47	155	g	25		12
B457	Cereal/Spec.	Hot oat cereal, 30 g, honey flavor (UK), prepared with 125 mL skim milk	47	155	g	26		12
B472	Cereal/Spec.	Wheat Cereal biscuit 30 g, wheat based, consumed with 125 mL skim milk (UK)	47	155	g	26		12
B464	Cereal/Spec.	Muesli, Wheat free, Pertwee Farm's, (UK),	49	30	g	19		9

FIBRE

REF#	CATEGORY	FOOD	GI	SERV	UM	CARB	FIBRE	GL
		consumed with semi-skimmed milk						
B472.1	Cereal/Spec.	Wheat Cereal biscuit, consumed with 125 mL skim milk, mean of four foods	50	155	g	27		13
B471	Cereal/Spec.	Wheat Cereal biscuit 30 g, honey flavor, consumed with 125 mL skim milk (UK)	52	155	g	27		14
B453	Cereal/Spec.	Honey Crunch cereal 30 g, consumed with 125 mL skim milk (UK)	54	155	g	30		16
B470	Cereal/Spec.	Wheat Cereal biscuit 30 g, fruit flavor, consumed with 125 mL skim milk (UK)	56	155	g	27		15
B450	Cereal/Spec.	Cereal flakes with fruit (UK)30 g), consumed with 125 mL skim milk (UK)UK)	57	155	g	29		16
B451	Cereal/Spec.	Cocoa Crunch cereal 30 g with 125 mL skim milk (UK)	58	155	g	28		16
B467	Cereal/Spec.	Precise, Sainsbury's, (UK), with semi-skimmed milk	59	30	g	24		14
B462	Cereal/Spec.	Muesli, Original, Sainsbury's, (UK), consumed with semi-skimmed milk	60	30	g	19		11
B463	Cereal/Spec.	Muesli, Swiss, Sainsbury's, (UK), consumed with semi-skimmed milk	60	30	g	19		12
B466	Cereal/Spec.	Porridge, small oats, Sainsbury's, (UK), consumed with semi-skimmed milk	61	250	g	22		14
B452	Cereal/Spec.	Cornflakes, Sainsbury's, (UK) 30 g, consumed with 125 mL skim milk	65	30	g	25		16
B449	Cereal/Spec.	Branflakes, Sainsbury's, (UK), with semi-skimmed milk	76	30	g	20		15
B468	Cereal/Spec.	Rice Pops™, Sainsbury's, (UK), with semi-skimmed milk	80	30	g	25		20
B1180	Con. Meal	Cannelloni, spinach and ricotta (UK)	15	300	g	54		8

FIBRE

REF#	CATEGORY	FOOD	GI	SERV	UM	CARB	FIBRE	GL
B1210	Con. Meal	Lasagne, vegetarian (UK)	20	300	g	48		10
B1216	Con. Meal	Lasagne, Pasta bake, tomato and mozzarella (UK)	23	300	g	43		10
B1209	Con. Meal	Lasagne, type NS (UK)	25	300	g	30		8
B1214	Con. Meal	Lasagne, Mushroom stroganoff with rice (UK)	26	300	g	43		11
B1207	Con. Meal	Lasagne, meat, Healthy Living, chilled, (UK)	28	300	g	38		11
B1196	Con. Meal	Cumberland pie (UK)	29	300	g	37		11
B1208	Con. Meal	Lasagne, type NS, Finest, (UK)	34	300	g	31		10
B1185	Con. Meal	Chicken tikka masala and rice, convenience meal, Healthy Living, (UK)	34	300	g	60		21
B1205	Con. Meal	Lamb moussaka, prepared convenience meal, Finest, (UK)	35	300	g	27		10
B1195	Con. Meal	Cumberland fish pie (UK)	40	300	g	31		12
B1257	Con. Meal	Sweet and sour chicken with noodles, prepared convenience meal, Serves One, (UK)	41	300	g	52		21
B1200	Con. Meal	Fajitas, chicken (UK)	42	300	g	42		18
B1186	Con. Meal	Chilli beef noodles, prepared convenience meal, Finest, (UK)	42	300	g	46		19
B1181	Con. Meal	Chicken korma and peshwari rice, prepared meal,Finest, UK)	44	300	g	48		21
B1182	Con. Meal	Chicken korma and rice, convenience meal, Healthy Living, (UK)	45	300	g	48		21
B1258	Con. Meal	Tandoori chicken masala & rice convenience meal, Finest, (UK)	45	300	g	61		27
B1206	Con. Meal	Lasagne, beef, frozen (UK)	47	300	g	35		17
B1189	Con. Meal	Chow mein, chicken, convenience meal, Serves One, (UK)	47	300	g	38		18
B1253	Con. Meal	Steak and ale with cheddar mash potato convenience meal, Finest, (UK)	48	300	g	26		12

FIBRE

REF#	CATEGORY	FOOD	GI	SERV	UM	CARB	FIBRE	GL
B1173	Con. Meal	Beef and ale casserole, convenience meal Finest, (UK)	53	300	g	15		8
B1188	Con. Meal	Chow mein, chicken, convenience meal, Healthy Living, (UK)	55	300	g	23		13
B1249	Con. Meal	Sausages and mash potato, prepared convenience meal (UK)	61	300	g	40		25
B1194	Con. Meal	Cottage pie (UK)	65	300	g	34		22
B1251	Con. Meal	Shepherds pie, prepared convenience meal (UK)	66	300	g	44		29
B758	Dairy	Fromage Frais, yellow fruit: passionfruit and pineapple, Healthy Living, (UK)	18	100	g	7		1
B756	Dairy	Fromage Frais, yellow fruit: mandarin and orange, Healthy Living, (UK)	19	100	g	7		1
B752	Dairy	Fromage Frais, red fruit: blackcurrant Healthy Living, (UK)	22	100	g	7		2
B759	Dairy	Fromage Frais, yellow fruit: peach and apricot, Healthy Living, (UK)	22	100	g	7		1
B754	Dairy	Fromage Frais, red fruit: red cherry (UK)Healthy Living,	25	100	g	7		2
B757	Dairy	Fromage Frais, yellow fruit: mango and papaya, Healthy Living, (UK)	25	100	g	7		2
B796	Dairy	Milk, semi-skimmed, British Dairycrest, (UK)	25	250	mL	13		3
B750	Dairy	Crème fraiche dessert, peach, Finest, (UK)	28	150	g	23		7
B755	Dairy	Fromage Frais, red fruit: strawberry, Healthy Living, (UK)	29	100	g	7		2
B751	Dairy	Crème fraiche dessert, raspberry, Finest, (UK)	30	150	g	17		5
B753	Dairy	Fromage Frais, red fruit: raspberryHealthy Living, (UK)	31	100	g	13		2
B787	Dairy	Milk, Full-fat, pasteurised, fresh, organic, Arla, (UK)	34	250	mL	12		4
B797	Dairy	Milk, semi-skimmed, pasteurised, organic	34	250	mL	13		4

FIBRE

REF#	CATEGORY	FOOD	GI	SERV	UM	CARB	FIBRE	GL
		Arla, (UK)						
B789	Dairy	Milk, Full-fat, standardised homogenised, pasteurised, British Dairycrest, (UK)	46	250	mL	12		5
B818	Dairy	Milk, skimmed, pasteurised, British Dairycrest, (UK)	48	250	mL	13		6
B859	Dairy/Yoghurt	Yoghurt, summer fruit: apricot, Healthy Living Light, (UK)	11	200	g	13		1
B842	Dairy/Yoghurt	Yoghurt, black cherry, Finest, (UK)	17	200	g	14		2
B864	Dairy/Yoghurt	Yoghurt, tropical fruit: guava and passionfruit, Healthy Living Light, (UK)	24	200	g	12		3
B860	Dairy/Yoghurt	Yoghurt, summer fruit: peach and vanilla, Healthy Living Light, (UK)	26	200	g	13		3
B866	Dairy/Yoghurt	Yoghurt, tropical fruit: peach and apricot, Healthy Living Light, (UK)	27	200	g	13		3
B861	Dairy/Yoghurt	Yoghurt, summer fruit: raspberry, Healthy Living Light, (UK)	28	200	g	12		3
B850	Dairy/Yoghurt	Yoghurt, peach & apricot, Healthy Living Light, (UK)	28	200	g	17		5
B857	Dairy/Yoghurt	Yoghurt, strawberry, Healthy Living Light, (UK)	30	200	g	16		5
B920	Dairy/Yoghurt	Yoghurt, Probiotic drink, orange (UK)	30	250	mL	34		10
B865	Dairy/Yoghurt	Yoghurt, tropical fruit: mango, Healthy Living Light, (UK)	32	200	g	13		4
B856	Dairy/Yoghurt	Yoghurt, Scottish raspberry, Finest, (UK)	32	200	g	40		13
B885	Dairy/Yoghurt	Yoghurt, Low-fat, raspberry (UK)	34	200	g	28		10
B921	Dairy/Yoghurt	Yoghurt, Probiotic drink, original (UK)	34	250	mL	31		11
B868	Dairy/Yoghurt	Yoghurt, Valencia orange, Finest, (UK)	34	200	g	33		11

FIBRE

REF#	CATEGORY	FOOD	GI	SERV	UM	CARB	FIBRE	GL
B853	Dairy/Yoghurt	Yoghurt, red fruit: Morello cherry, Healthy Living Light, (UK)	35	200	g	12		4
B895	Dairy/Yoghurt	Yoghurt, low fat, natural (UK)	35	200	g	35		12
B862	Dairy/Yoghurt	Yoghurt, summer fruit: strawberry, Healthy Living Light, (UK)	36	200	g	13		5
B847	Dairy/Yoghurt	Yoghurt, Greek style, honey topped (UK)	36	200	g	32		12
B854	Dairy/Yoghurt	Yoghurt, red fruit: raspberry and black cherry, Healthy Living Light, (UK)	37	200	g	13		5
B846	Dairy/Yoghurt	Yoghurt, Devonshire fudge, Finest, (UK)	37	200	g	34		13
B867	Dairy/Yoghurt	Yoghurt, tropical pineapple, Healthy Living Light, (UK)	38	200	g	13		5
B863	Dairy/Yoghurt	Yoghurt, toffee, Healthy Living Light, (UK)	41	200	g	16		7
B882	Dairy/Yoghurt	Yoghurt, Low-fat, black cherry (UK)	41	200	g	28		11
B858	Dairy/Yoghurt	Yoghurt, strawberry and cream, Finest, (UK)	41	200	g	38		16
B855	Dairy/Yoghurt	Yoghurt, red fruit: raspberry and cranberry, Healthy Living Light, (UK)	42	200	g	27		11
B881	Dairy/Yoghurt	Yoghurt, Low-fat, apricot (UK)	42	200	g	28		12
B849	Dairy/Yoghurt	Yoghurt, orange blossom, Finest, (UK)	42	200	g	40		17
B852	Dairy/Yoghurt	Yoghurt, raspberry, Healthy Living Light, (UK)	43	200	g	16		7
B908	Dairy/Yoghurt	Yoghurt, probiotic, prune (UK)	44	200	g	29		13
B909	Dairy/Yoghurt	Yoghurt, probiotic, raspberry (UK)	45	200	g	29		13
B869	Dairy/Yoghurt	Yoghurt, vanilla, Healthy Living Light, (UK)	47	200	g	14		7
B910.1	Dairy/Yoghurt	Yoghurt, probiotic, mean of three foods	47	200	g	29		14
B845	Dairy/Yoghurt	Yoghurt, champagne rhubarb, Finest, (UK)	49	200	g	38		19
B910	Dairy/Yoghurt	Yoghurt, probiotic, strawberry (UK)	52	200	g	29		15
B883	Dairy/Yoghurt	Yoghurt, Low-fat,	53	200	g	29		15

FIBRE

REF#	CATEGORY	FOOD	GI	SERV	UM	CARB	FIBRE	GL
		hazelnut (UK)						
B870	Dairy/Yoghurt	Yoghurt, white peach, Finest, (UK)	54	200	g	32		17
B884	Dairy/Yoghurt	Yoghurt, Low-fat, peach melba, Value, (UK)	56	200	g	28		16
B919	Dairy/Yoghurt	Yoghurt, Probiotic drink, cranberry (UK)	56	250	mL	31		17
B851	Dairy/Yoghurt	Yoghurt, peach melba, Value, (UK)	57	200	g	32		18
B886	Dairy/Yoghurt	Yoghurt, Low-fat, strawberry (UK)	61	200	g	30		18
B844	Dairy/Yoghurt	Yoghurt, bourbon vanilla, Finest, (UK)	64	200	g	32		20
B843	Dairy/Yoghurt	Yoghurt, black cherry, Healthy Living Light, (UK)	67	200	g	12		8
B848	Dairy/Yoghurt	Yoghurt, lemon curd, Finest, (UK)	67	200	g	45		30
B630	Digestive	Digestives (UK)	39	25	g	16		6
A318	Digestive	Digestives gluten-free, maize starch, Nutricia Dietary Care Ltd Redish Stockport (UK)	58	25	g	17		10
B951	Fruit	Apricots, dried, ready to eat (UK)	31	60	g	22		7
B952	Fruit	Apricots, dried, ready to eat, bite size (UK)	32	60	g	22		7
B1008	Fruit	Peach, dried (UK)	35	60	g	22		8
B1012	Fruit	Pear, dried (UK)	43	60	g	27		12
B1030	Fruit	Sultanas, Value, (UK)	56	60	g	42		23
B1031	Fruit	Sultanas (UK)	58	60	g	42		24
B992	Fruit	Mixed fruit, dried, Value, (UK)	60	60	g	41		24
B492	Grain	Barley, pearled, boiled 60 min (UK)	35	150	g	42		15
B557	Grain	Rice, Basmati, white, boiled, Sainsbury's, (UK)	43	150	g	43		18
B532	Grain	Rice, American, easy-cook rice, Sainsbury's, (UK)	49	150	g	46		22
B524	Grain	Long grain, white, pre-cooked, microwaved 2 min, Express Rice, plain, Uncle Ben's, Masterfoods, (UK)	52	150	g	37		19

FIBRE

REF#	CATEGORY	FOOD	GI	SERV	UM	CARB	FIBRE	GL
A280	Grain	Long grain white precooked microwaved 2 min, Express Rice plain Uncle Ben's; King's Lynn Norfolk (UK)	52	150	g	37		19
B565	Grain	Rice, Precooked basmati rice in pouch, white, reheated in microwave, Uncle Ben's Express® Masterfoods, (UK)	57	150	g	41		24
A297	Grain	Precooked basmati rice in pouch white reheated in microwave, Uncle Ben's Express; Masterfoods. Kings Lynn Norfolk (UK)	57	150	g	41		24
B564	Grain	Rice, Basmati, easy-cook rice, boiled, Sainsbury's, (UK)	68	150	g	41		28
B558	Grain/Spec.	Rice, Basmati, white, boiled 12 min, Value, (UK)	52	150	g	28		15
B558	Grain/Spec.	Rice, Basmati, white, boiled 12 min, Value, (UK)	52	150	g	28		15
B559	Grain/Spec.	Rice, Basmati, white, organic, boiled 10 min (UK)	57	150	g	40		23
B563	Grain/Spec.	Rice, Basmati, easy cook, white, boiled 9 min (UK)	67	150	g	42		28
B562	Grain/Spec.	Rice, Basmati, white, boiled 8 min (UK)	69	150	g	40		28
B1066	Infant Foods	Apple, apricot and banana cereal, Robinsons first Tastes from 4 months, Nutricia, Wells, (UK)	56	75	g	13		7
A447.1	Infant foods	Apple apricot and banana cereal6, Robinsons First Tastes from 4 months, Nutricia Wells, (UK)	56	75	g	13		11
B1067	Infant Foods	Creamed rice porridge, Robinsons first Tastes from 4 months, Nutricia, Wells, (UK)	59	75	g	9		5
A447.2	Infant foods	Creamed porridge, Robinsons First Tastes from 4 months, Nutricia	59	75	g	9		5

FIBRE

REF#	CATEGORY	FOOD	GI	SERV	UM	CARB	FIBRE	GL
		Wells (UK)						
B1068	Infant Foods	Rice pudding, Robinsons first Tastes from 4 months, Nutricia, Wells, (UK)	59	75	g	11		6
A447.3	Infant foods	Rice pudding, Robinsons First Tastes from 4 months (Nutricia Wells UK)	59	75	g	11		6
B1153	Meal Repl. & Weight Mgmt.	SlimFast® Garden vegetable soup with peppers and croutons, SlimFast Foods Ltd, UK)	20	250	mL	27		5
B1131	Meal Repl. & Weight Mgmt.	Chocolate weight management drink (UK)	23	250	mL	18		4
B1149	Meal Repl. & Weight Mgmt.	SlimFast® chocolate meal replacement bar SlimFast Foods Ltd, UK)	27	50	g	23		6
B1129	Meal Repl. & Weight Mgmt.	Chocolate, lactose-free, weight management drink (UK)	29	250	mL	19		6
B1146	Meal Repl. & Weight Mgmt.	Lemon weight management bar (UK)	32	50	g	21		7
B1152	Meal Repl. & Weight Mgmt.	SlimFast® Strawberry Supreme ready-to-drink shake, SlimFast Foods Ltd, UK)	33	250	mL	30		10
B1151	Meal Repl. & Weight Mgmt.	SlimFast® Double Chocolate meal replacement powder, prepared with skim milk, SlimFast Foods Ltd, UK)	36	50	g	46		17
B1132	Meal Repl. & Weight Mgmt.	Chocolate weight management drink (UK)	39	250	mL	18		7
B1147	Meal Repl. & Weight Mgmt.	Malt toffee weight management bar (UK)	43	50	g	24		10
B1150	Meal Repl. & Weight Mgmt.	SlimFast® Chocolate Muesli snack bar, SlimFast Foods Ltd, UK)	49	50	g	32		16
B1154	Meal Repl. & Weight Mgmt.	SlimFast® Pasta Florentina meal, SlimFast Foods, UK)	53	250	g	34		12
B1148	Meal Repl. & Weight Mgmt.	SlimFast® chocolate caramel meal replacement bar, SlimFast Foods Ltd, Slough, Berks, UK)	54	50	g	33		18
B1322	Nuts	Mixed nuts and raisins	21	50	g	16		3

FIBRE

REF#	CATEGORY	FOOD	GI	SERV	UM	CARB	FIBRE	GL
		(UK)						
B1323	Nuts	Mixed nuts, roasted and salted (UK)	24	50	g	17		4
B1318	Nuts	Cashew nuts (UK)	25	50	g	12		3
B1319	Nuts	Cashew nuts, organic, roasted and salted (UK)	25	50	g	12		3
B1320	Nuts	Cashew nut halves (UK)	27	50	g	10		3
B1321	Nuts	Cashew nuts, roasted and salted (UK)	27	50	g	10		3
B1383	Pasta	Tagliatelle, egg pasta, boiled in water for 7 min (UK)	46	180	g	44		20
B1333	Pasta	Fusilli pasta twists, tricolour, dry pasta, boiled 10 min in unsalted water (UK)	51	180	g	45		23
B1343	Pasta	Lasagne, egg, verdi, dry pasta, boiled in unsalted water for 10 min (UK)	52	180	g	45		23
B1342	Pasta	Lasagne, egg, dry pasta, boiled in unsalted water for 10 min(UK)	53	180	g	43		23
B1343.1	Pasta	Lasagne, egg, verdi, boiled in unsalted water for 10 min, mean of three studies	53	180	g	45		24
B1335	Pasta	Gluten-free pasta, maize starch, boiled 8 min (UK)	54	180	g	42		23
A522	Pasta	Gluten-free pasta maize starch boiled 8 min (UK)	54	180	g	42		22
B1384	Pasta	Tagliatelle, egg, boiled, Sainsbury's, UK)	54	180	g	44		24
B1332	Pasta	Fusilli pasta twists, dry pasta, boiled in 10 min in unsalted water (UK)	54	180	g	48		26
B1334	Pasta	Fusilli pasta twists, wholewheat, dry pasta, boiled 10 min in unsalted water (UK)	55	180	g	41		23
B1334.1	Pasta	Fusilli pasta, twists, mean of four studies	55	180	g	46		25
B1341	Pasta	Lasagne sheets, dry pasta, boiled in unsalted water for 10 min, Value, UK)	55	180	g	47		26
B1331	Pasta	Fusilli pasta twists, Tesco Stores Ltd, UK), boiled 10 min in salted	61	180	g	48		29

FIBRE

REF#	CATEGORY	FOOD	GI	SERV	UM	CARB	FIBRE	GL
		water (UK)						
B1218	Pasta/Spec.	Fusilli pasta twists, Tesco Stores Ltd, UK), boiled 10 min in salted water, served with cheddar cheese (UK)	27			48		13
B1217	Pasta/Spec.	Fusilli pasta twists, Tesco Stores Ltd, UK), boiled 10 min in salted water, served with canned tuna (UK)	28			48		13
B1219	Pasta/Spec.	Fusilli pasta twists, Tesco Stores Ltd, UK), boiled 10 min in salted water, served with chilli con carne (UK)	40			48		19
B1410	Snack	Fruit and nut mix, Finest, UK)	15	50	g	24		4
B1412	Snack	Apricot and Almond bar (UK)	34	30	g	15		5
B743	Snack	Crackers, Wholewheat with pumpkin and thyme (UK)UK)	36	25	g	15		6
B716	Snack	Crackers, Choice grain (UK)	49	25	g	16		8
B1499	Snack	Tropical fruit and nut mix, Finest, UK)	49	50	g	28		14
B744	Snack	Crackers, Wholewheat sticks, crunchy, yeast extract flavored (UK)	50	25	g	14		7
B742	Snack	Crackers, Wholegrain with sesame seeds and rosemary (UK)	53	25	g	16		8
B734	Snack	Crackers, Rye with sesame (UK)	57	25	g	16		9
B733	Snack	Crackers, Rye with oats (UK)	64	25	g	16		10
B1543	Soup	Garden vegetable soup with peppers and croutons, SlimFast®, SlimFast Foods Ltd, Slough, Berks, UK)	20	250	g	27		5
B1540	Soup	Chicken and mushroom soup (UK)	46	250	g	18		8
B1557	Soup	Vegetable soup (UK)	60	250	g	18		11
B1541	Soup	Chicken and mushroom soup (UK)	69	250	g	19		13

FIBRE

REF#	CATEGORY	FOOD	GI	SERV	UM	CARB	FIBRE	GL
A591.2	Sweetener	25 g Litesse III ultra bulking agent with polydextrose and sorbitol, (by weight), Danisco Sweeteners UK) vs 25 g carb in ref food (glucose).	4	10	g	10		0
A591.1	Sweetener	25 g Litesse II bulking agent with polydextrose and sorbitol (by weight), Danisco Sweeteners UK) vs 25 g. carb in ref food (glucose).	7	10	g	10		1
A593.3	Sweetener	25 g Xylitol (by weight), Danisco Sweeteners UK) vs ref food (glucose) with 25 g. carb. Mean of 2 studies	8	10	g	10		1
B1599	Sweetener	Lactose, 25 g portion, DBH, Poole, (UK)	48	10	g	10		5
B1640	Vegetable	Potato, Marfona, peeled, quartered, boiled 15 min in unsalted water (UK)UK)	56	150	g	32		18
B1642	Vegetable	Potato, Nicola, peeled, quartered, boiled 15 min (UK)	59	150	g	16		9
B1634	Vegetable	Potato, Charlotte, peeled, quartered, boiled 15 min (UK)	66	150	g	23		15
B1637	Vegetable	Potato, Estima, peeled, quartered, boiled 15 min (UK)	66	150	g	26		17
B1627	Vegetable	Potato, white, baked with skin, baked (UK)	69	150	g	27		19
B1639	Vegetable	Potato, King Edward potato, peeled, quartered, boiled 15 min in unsalted water (UK)	75	150	g	28		21
B1680	Vegetable	Potato, New, boiled (UK)	80	150	g	23		18
B1635	Vegetable	Potato, Charlotte, boiled (UK)	81	150	g	23		19
B1641	Vegetable	Potato, Maris Piper, peeled, quartered, boiled 15 min in unsalted water (UK)	85	150	g	29		25
B1674	Vegetable	Potato, Estima, microwaved 6 min then baked 10 min (UK)	93	150	g	26		24

FIBRE

REF#	CATEGORY	FOOD	GI	SERV	UM	CARB	FIBRE	GL
B1651	Vegetable	Potato, white, boiled (UK)	96	150	g	26		24
B1630	Vegetable	Potato, white, baked without skin, baked (UK)	98	150	g	27		26
B1672	Vegetable	Potato, Desiree, mashed (UK)	102	150	g	26		26
B1654	Vegetable/Spec.	Potato, Type NS, boiled in salted water, refrigerated, reheated, India)	23	150	g	34		8
B1228	Vegetable/Spec.	Potato, Estima, 50 g, microwaved 6 min then baked 10 min, served with cheddar cheese 62 g (UK)	39	112	g	26		10
B1226	Vegetable/Spec.	Potato, Estima, 50 g, microwaved 6 min then baked 10 min, served with baked beans, 89 g, (UK)	62	139	g	37		23
B1229	Vegetable/Spec.	Potato, Estima 50 g, microwaved 6 min then baked 10 min, served with chilli con carne, 63 g (UK)	75	113	g	31		23
B1227	Vegetable/Spec.	Potato, Estima, 50 g, microwaved 6 min then baked 10 min, served with canned tuna, 62 g (UK)	76	112	g	26		20

FIBRE

GLYCEMIC LOAD (GL)

REF#	CATEGORY	FOOD	GI	SERV	UM	CARB	FIBRE	GL
G	Beverage	Beer, wine, spirits (no GI, but can have carbs, depending on brand)	0			0		
G/USDA	Fruit	Avocado	0	120	g	11	8	0
G/USDA/#	Fruit	Boysenberries	40	120	g	14	6	0
G/USDA	Nuts	Almond meal flour	0	50	g	11	6	0
G/USDA	Nuts	Almonds	0	50	g	11	6	0
G/USDA	Nuts	Pecans	0	50	g	7	5	0
G/USDA	Nuts	Hazelnuts	0	50	g	8	5	0
G/USDA/#	Fruit	Blackberries	0	120	g	12	4	0
G/USDA	Nuts	Macadamia	0	50	g	7	4	0
G/USDA	Nuts	Walnuts	0	50	g	7	4	0
G/USDA	Vegetable	Spinach	0	150	g	4	3	0
H/USDA	Snack	Hummus, chickpea salad dip, commercially prepared	6	30	g	4	2	0
G/USDA	Vegetable	Green Leaf Lettuce	0	150	g	4	2	0
G/USDA	Beverage	Almond Milk, unsweetened	0	226	mL	1	1	0
G/USDA	Vegetable	Radish	40	30	g	1	1	0
G/USDA	Snack	Dill Pickle	40	28	g	0.6	0.3	0
USDA	Beverage	Coffee or tea, black, unsweetened	0			0	0	0
USDA	Beverage	Seltzer water, baking extract flavored, stevia sweetened	0			0	0	0
USDA	Beverage	Water	0			0	0	0
G/PKG	Beverage	Coconut Milk, unsweetened	0	240	mL	1	0	0

GLYCEMIC LOAD (GL)

REF#	CATEGORY	FOOD	GI	SERV	UM	CARB	FIBRE	GL
G/USDA	Meat, Fish & Poultry	All meat, fish, shellfish, poultry, including wild game or meats	0			0	0	0
G/USDA	Snack	Sardines, fish snacks, canned	0	95	g	0	0	0
G/USDA	Snack	Egg, hardboiled	0		g	1	0	0
PKG	Sweetener	Stevia extract	0			0	0	0
PKG	Sweetener	Stevia extract	0			0	0	0
PKG	Sweetener	Stevia	0	1	g	<1	0	0
PKG	Sweetener	Xylitol (1 packet)	7	2.04	g	2	0	0
A591.2	Sweetener	25 g Litesse III ultra bulking agent with polydextrose and sorbitol, (by weight), Danisco Sweeteners UK) vs 25 g carb in ref food (glucose).	4	10	g	10		0
G/USDA	Snack	Celery with Hummus	40	80	g	7	3	0
G/USDA/#	Fruit	Strawberries	40	120	g	3	2	1
USDA/#	Pulses	Cocoa powder, unsweetened	40	5	g	3	1	1
G/USDA	Vegetable	Watercress	40	120	g	2	1	1
G/USDA	Dairy	Creamed cottage cheese	30	226	g	4	0	1
PKG	Sweetener	Coconut palm sugar	35	4	g	4	0	1
PKG	Sweetener	Coconut palm sugar	35	4	g	4	0	1
B758	Dairy	Fromage Frais, yellow fruit: passionfruit and pineapple, Healthy Living, (UK)	18	100	g	7		1
B756	Dairy	Fromage Frais, yellow fruit: mandarin and orange, Healthy Living, (UK)	19	100	g	7		1
B759	Dairy	Fromage Frais, yellow fruit: peach and apricot, Healthy Living, (UK)	22	100	g	7		1
B859	Dairy/Yoghurt	Yoghurt, summer fruit: apricot, Healthy Living Light, (UK)	11	200	g	13		1
A591.1	Sweetener	25 g Litesse II bulking agent with polydextrose and sorbitol by weight,	7	10	g	10		1

GLYCEMIC LOAD (GL)

REF#	CATEGORY	FOOD	GI	SERV	UM	CARB	FIBRE	GL
		Danisco Sweeteners UK) vs 25 g. carb test food						
A593.3	Sweetener	25 g Xylitol (by weight), Danisco Sweeteners UK) vs ref food with 25 g. carb Mean of 2 studies	8	10	g	10		1
G/USDA/#	Fruit	Pomegranate	40	120	g	23	9	2
G/USDA	Pulses	Chickpea (Garbanzo Bean) flour	10	30	g	18	5	2
G/USDA	Vegetable	Collard greens	40	120	g	6	5	2
G/USDA/#	Fruit	Soursop	40	120	g	20	4	2
G/USDA	Vegetable	Asparagus	40	120	g	5	3	2
USDA/#	Pulses	Carob powder, unsweetened	40	6	g	5	2	2
G/USDA/#	Fruit	Rhubarb	40	120	g	5	2	2
G/USDA	Snack	Celery with Cashew Butter	40	80	g	10	2	2
G/USDA	Vegetable	Arugula	40	120	g	4	2	2
G/USDA	Vegetable	Celery	40	120	g	4	2	2
G/USDA	Vegetable	Swiss chard	40	120	g	4	2	2
G/USDA	Vegetable	Cauliflower	40	120	g	6	2	2
G/USDA	Vegetable	Cucumber	40	120	g	4	1	2
G/USDA	Vegetable	Mushrooms	40	120	g	4	1	2
G/USDA	Vegetable	Zucchini	40	120	g	4	1	2
G/USDA	Vegetable	Ginger root	40	28	g	5	1	2
G/USDA	Vegetable	Radiccio	40	120	g	5	1	2
G/USDA	Vegetable	Tomato	40	120	g	5	1	2
B752	Dairy	Fromage Frais, red fruit: blackcurrant Healthy Living, (UK)	22	100	g	7		2
B754	Dairy	Fromage Frais, red fruit: red cherry (UK)Healthy	25	100	g	7		2

GLYCEMIC LOAD (GL)

REF#	CATEGORY	FOOD	GI	SERV	UM	CARB	FIBRE	GL
		Living,						
B757	Dairy	Fromage Frais, yellow fruit: mango and papaya, Healthy Living, (UK)	25	100	g	7		2
B755	Dairy	Fromage Frais, red fruit: strawberry, Healthy Living, (UK)	29	100	g	7		2
B753	Dairy	Fromage Frais, red fruit: raspberryHealthy Living, (UK)	31	100	g	13		2
B842	Dairy/Yoghurt	Yoghurt, black cherry, Finest, (UK)	17	200	g	14		2
G/USDA	Bakery	Cookie, Ranger Cookies, (From recipe in Are You Sweet Enough Already?)	35	80	g	9	10	3
G/USDA	Vegetable	Mustard greens	40	120	g	7	9	3
G/USDA	Fruit	Raspberries	0	120	g	15	8	3
G/USDA	Vegetable	Eggplant	40	120	g	7	4	3
G/USDA	Vegetable	Kohlrabi	40	120	g	7	4	3
G/USDA/#	Vegetable	Olives	40	120	g	7	4	3
G/USDA	Vegetable	Green Beans	40	120	g	8	4	3
G/USDA	Vegetable	Okra	40	120	g	8	4	3
G/USDA	Vegetable	Cabbage	40	120	g	7	3	3
G/USDA	Vegetable	Broccoli	40	120	g	8	3	3
G/USDA/#	Fruit	Pineapple	40	120	g	16	2	3
G/USDA	Vegetable	Tomatillo	40	120	g	7	2	3
G/USDA/#	Fruit	Figs	40	28	g	8	1	3
G/USDA	Vegetable	Bok Choy	40	120	g	7	1	3
G/USDA	Vegetable	Garlic	40	28	g	8	1	3
B1128	Pulses	Split peas, yellow, dried, soaked overnight, boiled 55 min (UK)	25	150	g	13		3

GLYCEMIC LOAD (GL)

REF#	CATEGORY	FOOD	GI	SERV	UM	CARB	FIBRE	GL
B796	Dairy	Milk, semi-skimmed, British Dairycrest, (UK)	25	250	mL	13		3
B864	Dairy/Yoghurt	Yoghurt, tropical fruit: guava and passionfruit, Healthy Living Light, (UK)	24	200	g	12		3
B860	Dairy/Yoghurt	Yoghurt, summer fruit: peach and vanilla, Healthy Living Light, (UK)	26	200	g	13		3
B866	Dairy/Yoghurt	Yoghurt, tropical fruit: peach and apricot, Healthy Living Light, (UK)	27	200	g	13		3
B861	Dairy/Yoghurt	Yoghurt, summer fruit: raspberry, Healthy Living Light, (UK)	28	200	g	12		3
B1322	Nuts	Mixed nuts and raisins (UK)	21	50	g	16		3
B1318	Nuts	Cashew nuts (UK)	25	50	g	12		3
B1319	Nuts	Cashew nuts, organic, roasted and salted (UK)	25	50	g	12		3
B1320	Nuts	Cashew nut halves (UK)	27	50	g	10		3
B1321	Nuts	Cashew nuts, roasted and salted (UK)	27	50	g	10		3
G/USDA/#	Fruit	Rose hips	40	28	g	11	7	4
G/USDA	Vegetable	Grape leaves	40	60	g	10	7	4
G/USDA	Vegetable	Jicama	40	120	g	11	6	4
G/USDA/#	Fruit	Persimmon	40	120	g	41	4	4
G/USDA	Vegetable	Dandelion greens	40	120	g	11	4	4
G/USDA/#	Fruit	Lychee	40	120	g	20	2	4
G/USDA	Vegetable	Bell pepper	40	120	g	11	2	4
G/USDA	Vegetable	Kale	40	120	g	11	2	4
G/USDA	Vegetable	Onion	40	120	g	11	2	4
G/USDA/#	Fruit	Cantaloupe	40	120	g	10	1	4
G/USDA/#	Fruit	Honeydew	40	120	g	11	1	4

GLYCEMIC LOAD (GL)

REF#	CATEGORY	FOOD	GI	SERV	UM	CARB	FIBRE	GL
B1115	Pulses	Lentils, red, split, dried, boiled 25 min (UK)	21	150	g	18		4
B474	Cereal	Breakfast Cereal bar, hazelnut flavor (UK)	33	30	g	11		4
B787	Dairy	Milk, Full-fat, pasteurised, fresh, organic, Arla, (UK)	34	250	mL	12		4
B797	Dairy	Milk, semi-skimmed, pasteurised, organic Arla, (UK)	34	250	mL	13		4
B865	Dairy/Yoghurt	Yoghurt, tropical fruit: mango, Healthy Living Light, (UK)	32	200	g	13		4
B853	Dairy/Yoghurt	Yoghurt, red fruit: Morello cherry, Healthy Living Light, (UK)	35	200	g	12		4
B1131	Meal Repl. & Weight Mgmt.	Chocolate weight management drink (UK)	23	250	mL	18		4
B1323	Nuts	Mixed nuts, roasted and salted (UK)	24	50	g	17		4
B1410	Snack	Fruit and nut mix, Finest, UK)	15	50	g	24		4
USDA/#	Fruit	Passionfruit	40	120	g	28	12	5
G/USDA	Snack	Chocolado Parfait with a Cherry, (From recipe in Are You Sweet Enough Already?)	40	113	g	12	6	5
G/USDA	Vegetable	Artichoke	40	120	g	13	6	5
G/USDA	Fruit	Blueberries	29	120	g	17	3	5
G/USDA	Vegetable	Beet greens	40	120	g	12	3	5
G/USDA/#	Fruit	Mulberries	40	120	g	12	2	5
G/USDA/#	Fruit	Apricot	40	120	g	13	2	5
G/USDA/#	Fruit	Papaya	40	120	g	13	2	5
G/USDA/#	Fruit	Plum	40	120	g	13	2	5
B1090	Pulses	Butter Beans, dried, soaked overnight, boiled 50 min (UK)	26	150	g	20		5
B1270	Bread/Spec.	White bread 30 g, toasted, served with cheddar cheese 36 g, Hovis, (UK)	35	66	g	15		5

GLYCEMIC LOAD (GL)

REF#	CATEGORY	FOOD	GI	SERV	UM	CARB	FIBRE	GL
B228	Bread/Spec.	White bread, prepared with a 10 min prove and a second 2 min proving low loaf volume) (UK)	38	30	g	13		5
B475	Cereal	Breakfast Cereal bar, orange flavor (UK)	33	30	g	14		5
B312	Cereal	Bran cereal, high fiber (UK)	43	30	g	12		5
B751	Dairy	Crème fraiche dessert, raspberry, Finest, (UK)	30	150	g	17		5
B789	Dairy	Milk, Full-fat, standardised homogenised, pasteurised, British Dairycrest, (UK)	46	250	mL	12		5
B850	Dairy/Yoghurt	Yoghurt, peach & apricot, Healthy Living Light, (UK)	28	200	g	17		5
B857	Dairy/Yoghurt	Yoghurt, strawberry, Healthy Living Light, (UK)	30	200	g	16		5
B862	Dairy/Yoghurt	Yoghurt, summer fruit: strawberry, Healthy Living Light, (UK)	36	200	g	13		5
B854	Dairy/Yoghurt	Yoghurt, red fruit: raspberry and black cherry, Healthy Living Light, (UK)	37	200	g	13		5
B867	Dairy/Yoghurt	Yoghurt, tropical pineapple, Healthy Living Light, (UK)	38	200	g	13		5
B1067	Infant Foods	Creamed rice porridge, Robinsons first Tastes from 4 months, Nutricia, Wells, (UK)	59	75	g	9		5
A447.2	Infant foods	Creamed porridge, Robinsons First Tastes from 4 months, Nutricia Wells (UK)	59	75	g	9		5
B1153	Meal Repl. & Weight Mgmt.	SlimFast® Garden vegetable soup with peppers and croutons, SlimFast Foods Ltd, UK)	20	250	mL	27		5
B1412	Snack	Apricot and Almond bar (UK)	34	30	g	15		5
B1543	Soup	Garden vegetable soup with peppers and croutons, SlimFast®, SlimFast Foods Ltd,	20	250	g	27		5

GLYCEMIC LOAD (GL)

REF#	CATEGORY	FOOD	GI	SERV	UM	CARB	FIBRE	GL
		Slough, Berks, UK)						
B1599	Sweetener	Lactose, 25 g portion, DBH, Poole, (UK)	48	10	g	10		5
G/USDA	Vegetable	Wheatgrass	40	30	g	16	8	6
G/USDA/#	Fruit	Cranberries	40	120	g	14	6	6
G/USDA/#	Fruit	Kiwi	40	120	g	18	4	6
H/USDA	Snack	Microwave popcorn plain, average	55	20	g	11	3	6
G/USDA/#	Fruit	Cherries, red	40	120	g	14	2	6
B278	Bread	Seeded bread (UK)	49	30	g	11		6
B200	Bread/Spec.	White wheat flour bread with added wheatgerm and fiber with oat fiber (UK) (Italy)	59	30	g	12		6
B473	Cereal	Breakfast Cereal bar, cranberry flavor (UK)	42	30	g	15		6
B818	Dairy	Milk, skimmed, pasteurised, British Dairycrest, (UK)	48	250	mL	13		6
B630	Digestive	Digestives (UK)	39	25	g	16		6
B1068	Infant Foods	Rice pudding, Robinsons first Tastes from 4 months, Nutricia, Wells, (UK)	59	75	g	11		6
A447.3	Infant foods	Rice pudding, Robinsons First Tastes from 4 months (Nutricia Wells UK)	59	75	g	11		6
B1149	Meal Repl. & Weight Mgmt.	SlimFast® chocolate meal replacement bar SlimFast Foods Ltd, UK)	27	50	g	23		6
B1129	Meal Repl. & Weight Mgmt.	Chocolate, lactose-free, weight management drink (UK)	29	250	mL	19		6
B743	Snack	Crackers, Wholewheat with pumpkin and thyme (UK)UK)	36	25	g	15		6
G/USDA/#	Fruit	Guava	40	120	g	17	6	7
G/USDA	Vegetable	Turmeric root	40	28	g	18	6	7

GLYCEMIC LOAD (GL)

REF#	CATEGORY	FOOD	GI	SERV	UM	CARB	FIBRE	GL
G/USDA/#	Fruit	Mandarin	40	120	g	16	2	7
G/USDA/#	Fruit	Tangerine	40	120	g	16	2	7
G/USDA/#	Fruit	Mango	40	120	g	18	2	7
G/USDA	Vegetable	Leek	40	120	g	17	2	7
PKG	Sweetener	Blackstrap molasses	55	15	mL	13	0	7
B699	Bakery	Cookie, Rich Tea (UK)	40	25	g	18		7
B676	Bakery	Cookie, Oat biscuit (UK)	45	25	g	15		7
B188	Bread	White wheat flour bread, toasted, Hovis, (UK)	50	41	g	15		7
B256	Bread	Crusty malted wheat bread, Finest, (UK)	52	30	g	13		7
B273	Bread	Multiseed bread (UK)	54	30	g	12		7
B234	Bread	Wholemeal whole wheat, wheat flour bread Hovis, (UK)	68	30	g	11		7
B194	Bread/Spec.	White wheat flour bread, homemade, frozen, defrosted	54	30	g	13		7
B750	Dairy	Crème fraiche dessert, peach, Finest, (UK)	28	150	g	23		7
B863	Dairy/Yoghurt	Yoghurt, toffee, Healthy Living Light, (UK)	41	200	g	16		7
B852	Dairy/Yoghurt	Yoghurt, raspberry, Healthy Living Light, (UK)	43	200	g	16		7
B869	Dairy/Yoghurt	Yoghurt, vanilla, Healthy Living Light, (UK)	47	200	g	14		7
B951	Fruit	Apricots, dried, ready to eat (UK)	31	60	g	22		7
B952	Fruit	Apricots, dried, ready to eat, bite size (UK)	32	60	g	22		7
B1066	Infant Foods	Apple, apricot and banana cereal, Robinsons first Tastes from 4 months, Nutricia, Wells, (UK)	56	75	g	13		7
B1146	Meal Repl. & Weight Mgmt.	Lemon weight management bar (UK)	32	50	g	21		7
B1132	Meal Repl. & Weight Mgmt.	Chocolate weight management drink (UK)	39	250	mL	18		7
B744	Snack	Crackers, Wholewheat sticks, crunchy, yeast extract flavored (UK)	50	25	g	14		7

GLYCEMIC LOAD (GL)

REF#	CATEGORY	FOOD	GI	SERV	UM	CARB	FIBRE	GL
A749/USDA	South American	Wheat tortilla (Mexican)	30	50	g	26	5	8
G/USDA	Bakery	Chocolate Black Bean Cake (From recipe in Are You Sweet Enough Already?)	40	80	g	19	4	8
B296	Bread	Pita bread, unleavened, wholemeal (UK)	56	30	g	14		8
B172	Bread	White flour (UK)	59	30	g	13		8
B190.1	Bread	White wheat flour bread, toasted, mean of three studies	60	30	g	13		8
B189	Bread	White wheat flour bread, fresh, toasted British Bakeries Ltd, (UK)	63	40	g	12		8
B245	Bread	Wholemeal flour, stoneground whole wheat, Waitrose,(UK)	66	30	g	12		8
B111	Bread	Barley, Sunflower and barley bread Vogel's, (UK), course 80% kernels	70	30	g	12		8
B236	Bread	Wholemeal whole wheat, wheat flour bread Sainsbury's,(UK)	71	30	g	11		8
B239	Bread	Wholemeal whole wheat, wheat flour bread Hovis, (UK)	74	30	g	11		8
B267	Bread	Multigrain bread, Sainsbury's, (UK)	80	30	g	10		8
B193	Bread/Spec.	White wheat flour bread, frozen, defrosted and toasted, British Bakeries Ltd, (UK)	64	30	g	12		8
B192	Bread/Spec.	White wheat flour bread, homemade, frozen and defrosted (UK)	62	30	g	13		8
B1180	Con. Meal	Cannelloni, spinach and ricotta (UK)	15	300	g	54		8
B1209	Con. Meal	Lasagne, type NS (UK)	25	300	g	30		8
B1173	Con. Meal	Beef and ale casserole, convenience meal Finest, (UK)	53	300	g	15		8
B843	Dairy/Yoghurt	Yoghurt, black cherry, Healthy Living Light, (UK)	67	200	g	12		8
B1008	Fruit	Peach, dried (UK)	35	60	g	22		8
B716	Snack	Crackers, Choice grain	49	25	g	16		8

GLYCEMIC LOAD (GL)

REF#	CATEGORY	FOOD	GI	SERV	UM	CARB	FIBRE	GL
		(UK)						
B742	Snack	Crackers, Wholegrain with sesame seeds and rosemary (UK)	53	25	g	16		8
B1540	Soup	Chicken and mushroom soup (UK)	46	250	g	18		8
B1654	Vegetable/Spec.	Potato, Type NS, boiled in salted water, refrigerated, reheated, India)	23	150	g	34		8
G/USDA	Snack	Apple slices with peanut butter	38	120	g	23	5	9
G/USDA	Snack	Apple slices with peanut butter	38	120	g	23	5	9
B137	Bread	Fruit loaf, sliced (UK)	57	30	g	16		9
A356	Bread	Rye crispbread, High-fiber rye crispbread Ryvita Company Ltd Poole Dorset (UK)	59	25	g	15		9
B268	Bread	Multigrain batch bread (UK)	62	30	g	14		9
B149	Bread	Oatmeal batch bread (UK)	62	30	g	15		9
B190	Bread	White wheat flour bread, homemade, fresh, toasted (UK)	66	40	g	13		9
A78.1	Bread	Gluten-free fiber-enriched bread, unsliced gluten-free wheat starch soya bran) (UK)	69	30	g	13		9
A78.3	Bread	Gluten-free fiber-enriched bread, Mean of 2 studies	73	30	g	13		9
B229	Bread/Spec.	White bread, prepared with a 30 min prove and a second 12 min proving moderate loaf volume (UK)	72	30	g	13		9
B191	Bread/Spec.	White wheat flour bread, frozen and defrosted British Bakeries Ltd, (UK)	75	30	g	12		9
B342	Cereal	High-fiber cereal (UK)	52	30	g	17		9
B465	Cereal/Spec.	Porridge, jumbo oats (UK)Sainsbury's, UK), consumed with semi-skimmed milk	40	250	g	22		9

GLYCEMIC LOAD (GL)

REF#	CATEGORY	FOOD	GI	SERV	UM	CARB	FIBRE	GL
B455	Cereal/Spec.	Hot oat cereal, 30 g, cocoa flavor (UK) prepared with 125 mL skim milk	40	155	g	23		9
B460	Cereal/Spec.	Hot oat cereal, 30 g prepared with 125 mL skim milk (UK)	40	155	g	23		9
B464	Cereal/Spec.	Muesli, Wheat free, Pertwee Farm's, (UK), consumed with semi-skimmed milk	49	30	g	19		9
B734	Snack	Crackers, Rye with sesame (UK)	57	25	g	16		9
B1642	Vegetable	Potato, Nicola, peeled, quartered, boiled 15 min (UK)	59	150	g	16		9
G/USDA/#	Fruit	Plantain	40	120	g	38	3	10
B295	Bread	Pita bread, unleavened, white, mini (UK)	68	30	g	15		10
B175	Bread	White wheat flour bread, Sainsbury's, (UK)	70	30	g	14		10
A78.2	Bread	Gluten-free fiber-enriched bread, sliced gluten-free wheat starch soya bran (UK)	76	30	g	13		10
B313	Cereal	Branflakes, Healthy Living, (UK)	50	30	g	20		10
B376	Cereal	Muesli, wholewheat (UK)	56	30	g	18		10
B1210	Con. Meal	Lasagne, vegetarian (UK)	20	300	g	48		10
B1216	Con. Meal	Lasagne, Pasta bake, tomato and mozzarella (UK)	23	300	g	43		10
B1208	Con. Meal	Lasagne, type NS, Finest, (UK)	34	300	g	31		10
B1205	Con. Meal	Lamb moussaka, prepared convenience meal, Finest, (UK)	35	300	g	27		10
B920	Dairy/Yoghurt	Yoghurt, Probiotic drink, orange (UK)	30	250	mL	34		10
B885	Dairy/Yoghurt	Yoghurt, Low-fat, raspberry (UK)	34	200	g	28		10
A318	Digestive	Digestives gluten-free, maize starch, Nutricia Dietary Care Ltd Redish Stockport (UK)	58	25	g	17		10

GLYCEMIC LOAD (GL)

REF#	CATEGORY	FOOD	GI	SERV	UM	CARB	FIBRE	GL
B1152	Meal Repl. & Weight Mgmt.	SlimFast® Strawberry Supreme ready-to-drink shake, SlimFast Foods Ltd, UK)	33	250	mL	30		10
B1147	Meal Repl. & Weight Mgmt.	Malt toffee weight management bar (UK)	43	50	g	24		10
B733	Snack	Crackers, Rye with oats (UK)	64	25	g	16		10
B1228	Vegetable/Spec.	Potato, Estima, 50 g, microwaved 6 min then baked 10 min, served with cheddar cheese 62 g (UK)	39	112	g	26		10
G/USDA	Fruit	Banana, slightly under-ripe, yellow with green sections	42	120	g	25	3	11
A356	Bread	Rye crispbread Ryvita Company Ltd (UK)	63	25	g	18		11
A77.1	Bread	Gluten-free white bread gluten-free wheat starch (UK), Unsliced	71	30	g	15		11
B135	Bread	Fruit and cinnamon bread, Finest, (UK)	71	30	g	16		11
B180	Bread	White wheat flour bread, Hovis, (UK)	73	30	g	15		11
B183	Bread	White wheat flour bread, Hovis, (UK)	75	30	g	15		11
A77.3	Bread	Gluten-free white bread gluten-free wheat starch (UK), Mean of 2 studies	76	30	g	15		11
B184	Bread	White wheat flour flour bread Hovis Classic, British Bakeries Ltd, (UK)	87	30	g	12		11
B1269	Bread/Spec.	White bread 30 g, toasted, served with baked beans 51 g, Hovis, (UK)	50	81	g	21		11
B230	Bread/Spec.	White bread, prepared with a 60 min prove and a second 30 min proving moderate loaf volume (UK)	86	30	g	13		11
B355	Cereal	Muesli, Alpen original, made from steamed rolled oats with dried fruit and nuts, Weetabix, (UK)	55	30	g	19		11

GLYCEMIC LOAD (GL)

REF#	CATEGORY	FOOD	GI	SERV	UM	CARB	FIBRE	GL
B363	Cereal	Muesli, fruit and nut (UK)	59	30	g	18		11
B454	Cereal/Spec.	Hot oat cereal 30 g, berry flavor (UK) prepared with 125 mL skim milk	43	155	g	26		11
B460.1	Cereal/Spec.	Cereal, Hot oat cereal mean of seven foods prepared with 125 mL skim milk	46	155	g	24		11
B459	Cereal/Spec.	Hot oat cereal 30 g prepared with 125 mL skim milk	47	155	g	23		11
B462	Cereal/Spec.	Muesli, Original, Sainsbury's, (UK), consumed with semi-skimmed milk	60	30	g	19		11
B1214	Con. Meal	Lasagne, Mushroom stroganoff with rice (UK)	26	300	g	43		11
B1207	Con. Meal	Lasagne, meat, Healthy Living, chilled, (UK)	28	300	g	38		11
B1196	Con. Meal	Cumberland pie (UK)	29	300	g	37		11
B921	Dairy/Yoghurt	Yoghurt, Probiotic drink, original (UK)	34	250	mL	31		11
B868	Dairy/Yoghurt	Yoghurt, Valencia orange, Finest, (UK)	34	200	g	33		11
B882	Dairy/Yoghurt	Yoghurt, Low-fat, black cherry (UK)	41	200	g	28		11
B855	Dairy/Yoghurt	Yoghurt, red fruit: raspberry and cranberry, Healthy Living Light, (UK)	42	200	g	27		11
A447.1	Infant foods	Apple apricot and banana cereal6, Robinsons First Tastes from 4 months, Nutricia Wells, (UK)	56	75	g	13		11
B1557	Soup	Vegetable soup (UK)	60	250	g	18		11
A744/USDA	South American	Corn tortilla (Mexican)	52	50	g	24	1	12
B1111	Pulses	Red Kidney Beans, dried, soaked overnight, boiled 60 min (UK)	51	150	g	24		12
B265	Bread	Malt loaf, organic (UK)	59	30	g	21		12
A77.2	Bread	Gluten-free white bread gluten-free wheat starch) (UK), Sliced	80	30	g	15		12
B187	Bread	White wheat flour bread, homemade (UK)	89	30	g	13		12

GLYCEMIC LOAD (GL)

REF#	CATEGORY	FOOD	GI	SERV	UM	CARB	FIBRE	GL
B353	Cereal	Mini Wheats, whole wheat, Sainsbury's, (UK)	59	30	g	21		12
B359	Cereal	Muesli, Value, UK)	64	30	g	19		12
B458	Cereal/Spec.	Hot oat cereal 30 g, orchard fruit flavor (UK) prepared with 125 mL skim milk	5	155	g	25		12
B469	Cereal/Spec.	Wheat Cereal biscuit 30 g, cocoa flavor, consumed with 125 mL skim milk (UK)	46	155	g	27		12
B456	Cereal/Spec.	Hot oat cereal, 30 g, fruit flavor (UK) prepared with 125 mL skim milk	47	155	g	25		12
B457	Cereal/Spec.	Hot oat cereal, 30 g, honey flavor (UK), prepared with 125 mL skim milk	47	155	g	26		12
B472	Cereal/Spec.	Wheat Cereal biscuit 30 g, wheat based, consumed with 125 mL skim milk (UK)	47	155	g	26		12
B463	Cereal/Spec.	Muesli, Swiss, Sainsbury's, (UK), consumed with semi-skimmed milk	60	30	g	19		12
B1195	Con. Meal	Cumberland fish pie (UK)	40	300	g	31		12
B1253	Con. Meal	Steak and ale with cheddar mash potato convenience meal, Finest, (UK)	48	300	g	26		12
B895	Dairy/Yoghurt	Yoghurt, low fat, natural (UK)	35	200	g	35		12
B847	Dairy/Yoghurt	Yoghurt, Greek style, honey topped (UK)	36	200	g	32		12
B881	Dairy/Yoghurt	Yoghurt, Low-fat, apricot (UK)	42	200	g	28		12
B1012	Fruit	Pear, dried (UK)	43	60	g	27		12
B1154	Meal Repl. & Weight Mgmt.	SlimFast® Pasta Florentina meal, SlimFast Foods, UK)	53	250	g	34		12
B231	Bread/Spec.	White bread, prepared with a 40 min prove, a second 25 min proving and a third 50 min proving large loaf volume (UK)	100	30	g	13		13

GLYCEMIC LOAD (GL)

REF#	CATEGORY	FOOD	GI	SERV	UM	CARB	FIBRE	GL
B332	Cereal	Fruit and Fibre™, Sainsbury's, UK)	61	30	g	21		13
B334.1	Cereal	Fruit and Fibre, mean of three studies	65	30	g	21		13
B334	Cereal	Fruit and Fibre, Value, (UK)	68	30	g	20		13
B472.1	Cereal/Spec.	Wheat Cereal biscuit, consumed with 125 mL skim milk, mean of four foods	50	155	g	27		13
B1188	Con. Meal	Chow mein, chicken, convenience meal, Healthy Living, (UK)	55	300	g	23		13
B856	Dairy/Yoghurt	Yoghurt, Scottish raspberry, Finest, (UK)	32	200	g	40		13
B846	Dairy/Yoghurt	Yoghurt, Devonshire fudge, Finest, (UK)	37	200	g	34		13
B908	Dairy/Yoghurt	Yoghurt, probiotic, prune (UK)	44	200	g	29		13
B909	Dairy/Yoghurt	Yoghurt, probiotic, raspberry (UK)	45	200	g	29		13
B1218	Pasta/Spec.	Fusilli pasta twists, Tesco Stores Ltd, UK), boiled 10 min in salted water, served with cheddar cheese (UK)	27			48		13
B1217	Pasta/Spec.	Fusilli pasta twists, Tesco Stores Ltd, UK), boiled 10 min in salted water, served with canned tuna (UK)	28			48		13
B1541	Soup	Chicken and mushroom soup (UK)	69	250	g	19		13
B333	Cereal	Fruit and Fibre (UK)	67	30	g	21		14
B362	Cereal	Muesli, fruit (UK)	67	30	g	21		14
B441	Cereal	Wheat based cereal biscuit (UK) (Plain flaked wheat)	72	30	g	20		14
B471	Cereal/Spec.	Wheat Cereal biscuit 30 g, honey flavor, consumed with 125 mL skim milk (UK)	52	155	g	27		14
B467	Cereal/Spec.	Precise, Sainsbury's, (UK), with semi-skimmed milk	59	30	g	24		14
B466	Cereal/Spec.	Porridge, small oats, Sainsbury's, (UK), consumed with semi-	61	250	g	22		14

GLYCEMIC LOAD (GL)

REF#	CATEGORY	FOOD	GI	SERV	UM	CARB	FIBRE	GL
		skimmed milk						
B910.1	Dairy/Yoghurt	Yoghurt, probiotic, mean of three foods	47	200	g	29		14
B1499	Snack	Tropical fruit and nut mix, Finest, UK)	49	50	g	28		14
B470	Cereal/Spec.	Wheat Cereal biscuit 30 g, fruit flavor, consumed with 125 mL skim milk (UK)	56	155	g	27		15
B449	Cereal/Spec.	Branflakes, Sainsbury's, (UK), with semi-skimmed milk	76	30	g	20		15
B910	Dairy/Yoghurt	Yoghurt, probiotic, strawberry (UK)	52	200	g	29		15
B883	Dairy/Yoghurt	Yoghurt, Low-fat, hazelnut (UK)	53	200	g	29		15
B492	Grain	Barley, pearled, boiled 60 min (UK)	35	150	g	42		15
B558	Grain/Spec.	Rice, Basmati, white, boiled 12 min, Value, (UK)	52	150	g	28		15
B558	Grain/Spec.	Rice, Basmati, white, boiled 12 min, Value, (UK)	52	150	g	28		15
B1634	Vegetable	Potato, Charlotte, peeled, quartered, boiled 15 min (UK)	66	150	g	23		15
B1048	Beverage	Cranberry juice drink, Ocean Spray®, Gerber Ltd., Bridgewater, Somerset, (UK)	56	250	mL	29		16
A39	Beverage	Cranberry juice drink Ocean Spray, Gerber Ltd Bridgewater (UK)	56	250	mL	29		16
A402	Beverage	Cranberry juice drink, Ocean Spray; Gerber Ltd Bridgewater Somerset(UK)	56	250	mL	29		16
A142	Bread	Whole-wheat snack bread, Ryvita Co Ltd Poole Dorset (UK)	74	30	g	22		16
B453	Cereal/Spec.	Honey Crunch cereal 30 g, consumed with 125 mL skim milk (UK)	54	155	g	30		16
B450	Cereal/Spec.	Cereal flakes with fruit (UK)30 g), consumed with 125 mL skim milk (UK)UK)	57	155	g	29		16

GLYCEMIC LOAD (GL)

REF#	CATEGORY	FOOD	GI	SERV	UM	CARB	FIBRE	GL
B451	Cereal/Spec.	Cocoa Crunch cereal 30 g with 125 mL skim milk (UK)	58	155	g	28		16
B452	Cereal/Spec.	Cornflakes, Sainsbury's, (UK) 30 g, consumed with 125 mL skim milk	65	30	g	25		16
B858	Dairy/Yoghurt	Yoghurt, strawberry and cream, Finest, (UK)	41	200	g	38		16
B884	Dairy/Yoghurt	Yoghurt, Low-fat, peach melba, Value, (UK)	56	200	g	28		16
B1150	Meal Repl. & Weight Mgmt.	SlimFast® Chocolate Muesli snack bar, SlimFast Foods Ltd, UK)	49	50	g	32		16
B304	Cereal	Balance™, Sainsbury's, (UK)	74	30	g	23		17
B1206	Con. Meal	Lasagne, beef, frozen (UK)	47	300	g	35		17
B849	Dairy/Yoghurt	Yoghurt, orange blossom, Finest, (UK)	42	200	g	40		17
B870	Dairy/Yoghurt	Yoghurt, white peach, Finest, (UK)	54	200	g	32		17
B919	Dairy/Yoghurt	Yoghurt, Probiotic drink, cranberry (UK)	56	250	mL	31		17
B1151	Meal Repl. & Weight Mgmt.	SlimFast® Double Chocolate meal replacement powder, prepared with skim milk, SlimFast Foods Ltd, UK)	36	50	g	46		17
B1637	Vegetable	Potato, Estima, peeled, quartered, boiled 15 min (UK)	66	150	g	26		17
B397	Cereal	Porridge, organic, made from rolled oats (UK)	63	250	g	29		18
B361	Cereal	Muesli, Healthy Eating, (UK)	86	30	g	21		18
B1200	Con. Meal	Fajitas, chicken (UK)	42	300	g	42		18
B1189	Con. Meal	Chow mein, chicken, convenience meal, Serves One, (UK)	47	300	g	38		18
B851	Dairy/Yoghurt	Yoghurt, peach melba, Value, (UK)	57	200	g	32		18
B886	Dairy/Yoghurt	Yoghurt, Low-fat, strawberry (UK)	61	200	g	30		18
B557	Grain	Rice, Basmati, white, boiled, Sainsbury's, (UK)	43	150	g	43		18

GLYCEMIC LOAD (GL)

REF#	CATEGORY	FOOD	GI	SERV	UM	CARB	FIBRE	GL
B1148	Meal Repl. & Weight Mgmt.	SlimFast® chocolate caramel meal replacement bar, SlimFast Foods Ltd, Slough, Berks, UK)	54	50	g	33		18
B1640	Vegetable	Potato, Marfona, peeled, quartered, boiled 15 min in unsalted water (UK)UK)	56	150	g	32		18
B1680	Vegetable	Potato, New, boiled (UK)	80	150	g	23		18
B396	Cereal	Porridge made from rolled oats, Value, UK)	63	250	g	30		19
B1186	Con. Meal	Chilli beef noodles, prepared convenience meal, Finest, (UK)	42	300	g	46		19
B845	Dairy/Yoghurt	Yoghurt, champagne rhubarb, Finest, (UK)	49	200	g	38		19
B524	Grain	Long grain, white, pre-cooked, microwaved 2 min, Express Rice, plain, Uncle Ben's, Masterfoods, (UK)	52	150	g	37		19
A280	Grain	Long grain white precooked microwaved 2 min, Express Rice plain Uncle Ben's; King's Lynn Norfolk (UK)	52	150	g	37		19
B1219	Pasta/Spec.	Fusilli pasta twists, Tesco Stores Ltd, UK), boiled 10 min in salted water, served with chilli con carne (UK)	40			48		19
B1627	Vegetable	Potato, white, baked with skin, baked (UK)	69	150	g	27		19
B1635	Vegetable	Potato, Charlotte, boiled (UK)	81	150	g	23		19
B1264	Bread/Spec.	White bread roll with cheese (UK)	50	100	g	40		20
B398	Cereal	Porridge, made from rolled oats, Scottish (UK)	63	250	g	31		20
B468	Cereal/Spec.	Rice Pops™, Sainsbury's, (UK), with semi-skimmed milk	80	30	g	25		20
B844	Dairy/Yoghurt	Yoghurt, bourbon vanilla, Finest, (UK)	64	200	g	32		20
B1383	Pasta	Tagliatelle, egg pasta, boiled in water for 7 min (UK)	46	180	g	44		20

GLYCEMIC LOAD (GL)

REF#	CATEGORY	FOOD	GI	SERV	UM	CARB	FIBRE	GL
B1227	Vegetable/Spec.	Potato, Estima, 50 g, microwaved 6 min then baked 10 min, served with canned tuna, 62 g (UK)	76	112	g	26		20
B1185	Con. Meal	Chicken tikka masala and rice, convenience meal, Healthy Living, (UK)	34	300	g	60		21
B1257	Con. Meal	Sweet and sour chicken with noodles, prepared convenience meal, Serves One, (UK)	41	300	g	52		21
B1181	Con. Meal	Chicken korma and peshwari rice, prepared meal,Finest, UK)	44	300	g	48		21
B1182	Con. Meal	Chicken korma and rice, convenience meal, Healthy Living, (UK)	45	300	g	48		21
B1639	Vegetable	Potato, King Edward potato, peeled, quartered, boiled 15 min in unsalted water (UK)	75	150	g	28		21
B1194	Con. Meal	Cottage pie (UK)	65	300	g	34		22
B532	Grain	Rice, American, easy-cook rice, Sainsbury's, (UK)	49	150	g	46		22
A522	Pasta	Gluten-free pasta maize starch boiled 8 min (UK)	54	180	g	42		22
B325	Cereal	Cornflakes, Kellogg's, (UK)	93	30	g	25		23
B1030	Fruit	Sultanas, Value, (UK)	56	60	g	42		23
B559	Grain/Spec.	Rice, Basmati, white, organic, boiled 10 min (UK)	57	150	g	40		23
B1333	Pasta	Fusilli pasta twists, tricolour, dry pasta, boiled 10 min in unsalted water (UK)	51	180	g	45		23
B1343	Pasta	Lasagne, egg, verdi, dry pasta, boiled in unsalted water for 10 min (UK)	52	180	g	45		23
B1342	Pasta	Lasagne, egg, dry pasta, boiled in unsalted water for 10 min(UK)	53	180	g	43		23
B1335	Pasta	Gluten-free pasta, maize starch, boiled 8 min (UK)	54	180	g	42		23

GLYCEMIC LOAD (GL)

REF#	CATEGORY	FOOD	GI	SERV	UM	CARB	FIBRE	GL
B1334	Pasta	Fusilli pasta twists, wholewheat, dry pasta, boiled 10 min in unsalted water (UK)	55	180	g	41		23
B1226	Vegetable/Spec.	Potato, Estima, 50 g, microwaved 6 min then baked 10 min, served with baked beans, 89 g, (UK)	62	139	g	37		23
B1229	Vegetable/Spec.	Potato, Estima 50 g, microwaved 6 min then baked 10 min, served with chilli con carne, 63 g (UK)	75	113	g	31		23
B1031	Fruit	Sultanas (UK)	58	60	g	42		24
B992	Fruit	Mixed fruit, dried, Value, (UK)	60	60	g	41		24
B565	Grain	Rice, Precooked basmati rice in pouch, white, reheated in microwave, Uncle Ben's Express® Masterfoods, (UK)	57	150	g	41		24
A297	Grain	Precooked basmati rice in pouch white reheated in microwave, Uncle Ben's Express; Masterfoods. Kings Lynn Norfolk (UK)	57	150	g	41		24
B1343.1	Pasta	Lasagne, egg, verdi, boiled in unsalted water for 10 min, mean of three studies	53	180	g	45		24
B1384	Pasta	Tagliatelle, egg, boiled, Sainsbury's, UK)	54	180	g	44		24
B1674	Vegetable	Potato, Estima, microwaved 6 min then baked 10 min (UK)	93	150	g	26		24
B1651	Vegetable	Potato, white, boiled (UK)	96	150	g	26		24
B1249	Con. Meal	Sausages and mash potato, prepared convenience meal (UK)	61	300	g	40		25
B1334.1	Pasta	Fusilli pasta, twists, mean of four studies	55	180	g	46		25
B1641	Vegetable	Potato, Maris Piper, peeled, quartered, boiled 15 min in unsalted water (UK)	85	150	g	29		25

GLYCEMIC LOAD (GL)

REF#	CATEGORY	FOOD	GI	SERV	UM	CARB	FIBRE	GL
B1332	Pasta	Fusilli pasta twists, dry pasta, boiled in 10 min in unsalted water (UK)	54	180	g	48		26
B1341	Pasta	Lasagne sheets, dry pasta, boiled in unsalted water for 10 min, Value, UK)	55	180	g	47		26
B1630	Vegetable	Potato, white, baked without skin, baked (UK)	98	150	g	27		26
B1672	Vegetable	Potato, Desiree, mashed (UK)	102	150	g	26		26
B1258	Con. Meal	Tandoori chicken masala & rice convenience meal, Finest, (UK)	45	300	g	61		27
B564	Grain	Rice, Basmati, easy-cook rice, boiled, Sainsbury's, (UK)	68	150	g	41		28
B563	Grain/Spec.	Rice, Basmati, easy cook, white, boiled 9 min (UK)	67	150	g	42		28
B562	Grain/Spec.	Rice, Basmati, white, boiled 8 min (UK)	69	150	g	40		28
B1251	Con. Meal	Shepherds pie, prepared convenience meal (UK)	66	300	g	44		29
B1331	Pasta	Fusilli pasta twists, Tesco Stores Ltd, UK), boiled 10 min in salted water (UK)	61	180	g	48		29
B411	Cereal	Porridge, Instant oat cereal porridge prepared with water (UK)	83	250	g	36		30
B848	Dairy/Yoghurt	Yoghurt, lemon curd, Finest, (UK)	67	200	g	45		30
A24	Beverage	Lucozade original, sparkling glucose drink) Glaxo Wellcome Ltd Uxbridge UK)	95	250	mL	42		40

GLYCEMIC LOAD (GL)

CATEGORY

REF#	CATEGORY	FOOD	GI	SERV	UM	CARB	FIBRE	GL
G/USDA	Bakery	Chocolate Black Bean Cake (From recipe in Are You Sweet Enough Already?)	40	80	g	19	4	8
G/USDA	Bakery	Cookie, Ranger Cookies, (From recipe in Are You Sweet Enough Already?)	35	80	g	9	10	3
B699	Bakery	Cookie, Rich Tea (UK)	40	25	g	18		7
B676	Bakery	Cookie, Oat biscuit (UK)	45	25	g	15		7
USDA	Beverage	Coffee or tea, black, unsweetened	0			0	0	0
USDA	Beverage	Seltzer water, baking extract flavored, stevia sweetened	0			0	0	0
USDA	Beverage	Water	0			0	0	0
G/PKG	Beverage	Coconut Milk, unsweetened	0	240	mL	1	0	0
G/USDA	Beverage	Almond Milk, unsweetened	0	226	mL	1	1	0
G	Beverage	Beer, wine, spirits (no GI, but can have carbs, depending on brand)	0			0		
B1048	Beverage	Cranberry juice drink, Ocean Spray®, Gerber Ltd., Bridgewater, Somerset, (UK)	56	250	mL	29		16
A39	Beverage	Cranberry juice drink Ocean Spray, Gerber Ltd Bridgewater (UK)	56	250	mL	29		16
A402	Beverage	Cranberry juice drink, Ocean Spray; Gerber Ltd Bridgewater Somerset(UK)	56	250	mL	29		16
A24	Beverage	Lucozade original, sparkling glucose drink) Glaxo Wellcome Ltd Uxbridge UK)	95	250	mL	42		40
B278	Bread	Seeded bread (UK)	49	30	g	11		6
B188	Bread	White wheat flour bread, toasted, Hovis, (UK)	50	41	g	15		7
B256	Bread	Crusty malted wheat bread, Finest, (UK)	52	30	g	13		7

CATEGORY

REF#	CATEGORY	FOOD	GI	SERV	UM	CARB	FIBRE	GL
B273	Bread	Multiseed bread (UK)	54	30	g	12		7
B296	Bread	Pita bread, unleavened, wholemeal (UK)	56	30	g	14		8
B137	Bread	Fruit loaf, sliced (UK)	57	30	g	16		9
B172	Bread	White flour (UK)	59	30	g	13		8
A356	Bread	Rye crispbread, High-fiber rye crispbread Ryvita Company Ltd Poole Dorset (UK)	59	25	g	15		9
B265	Bread	Malt loaf, organic (UK)	59	30	g	21		12
B268	Bread	Multigrain batch bread (UK)	62	30	g	14		9
B149	Bread	Oatmeal batch bread (UK)	62	30	g	15		9
B189	Bread	White wheat flour bread, fresh, toasted British Bakeries Ltd, (UK)	63	40	g	12		8
A356	Bread	Rye crispbread Ryvita Company Ltd (UK)	63	25	g	18		11
B245	Bread	Wholemeal flour, stoneground whole wheat, Waitrose,(UK)	66	30	g	12		8
B190	Bread	White wheat flour bread, homemade, fresh, toasted (UK)	66	40	g	13		9
B234	Bread	Wholemeal whole wheat, wheat flour bread Hovis, (UK)	68	30	g	11		7
B295	Bread	Pita bread, unleavened, white, mini (UK)	68	30	g	15		10
A78.1	Bread	Gluten-free fiber-enriched bread, unsliced gluten-free wheat starch soya bran) (UK)	69	30	g	13		9
B111	Bread	Barley, Sunflower and barley bread Vogel's, (UK), course 80% kernels	70	30	g	12		8
B175	Bread	White wheat flour bread, Sainsbury's, (UK)	70	30	g	14		10
B236	Bread	Wholemeal whole wheat, wheat flour bread Sainsbury's,(UK)	71	30	g	11		8
A77.1	Bread	Gluten-free white bread gluten-free wheat starch (UK), Unsliced	71	30	g	15		11
B135	Bread	Fruit and cinnamon bread, Finest, (UK)	71	30	g	16		11

CATEGORY

REF#	CATEGORY	FOOD	GI	SERV	UM	CARB	FIBRE	GL
A78.3	Bread	Gluten-free fiber-enriched bread, Mean of 2 studies	73	30	g	13		9
B180	Bread	White wheat flour bread, Hovis, (UK)	73	30	g	15		11
B239	Bread	Wholemeal whole wheat, wheat flour bread Hovis, (UK)	74	30	g	11		8
A142	Bread	Whole-wheat snack bread, Ryvita Co Ltd Poole Dorset (UK)	74	30	g	22		16
B183	Bread	White wheat flour bread, Hovis, (UK)	75	30	g	15		11
A78.2	Bread	Gluten-free fiber-enriched bread, sliced gluten-free wheat starch soya bran (UK)	76	30	g	13		10
A77.3	Bread	Gluten-free white bread gluten-free wheat starch (UK), Mean of 2 studies	76	30	g	15		11
B267	Bread	Multigrain bread, Sainsbury's, (UK)	80	30	g	10		8
A77.2	Bread	Gluten-free white bread gluten-free wheat starch) (UK), Sliced	80	30	g	15		12
B184	Bread	White wheat flour flour bread Hovis Classic, British Bakeries Ltd, (UK)	87	30	g	12		11
B187	Bread	White wheat flour bread, homemade (UK)	89	30	g	13		12
B190.1	Bread/Spec.	White wheat flour bread, toasted, mean of three studies	60	30	g	13		8
B1270	Bread/Spec.	White bread 30 g, toasted, served with cheddar cheese 36 g, Hovis, (UK)	35	66	g	15		5
B228	Bread/Spec.	White bread, prepared with a 10 min prove and a second 2 min proving low loaf volume) (UK)	38	30	g	13		5
B1269	Bread/Spec.	White bread 30 g, toasted, served with baked beans 51 g, Hovis, (UK)	50	81	g	21		11
B1264	Bread/Spec.	White bread roll with cheese (UK)	50	100	g	40		20

CATEGORY

REF#	CATEGORY	FOOD	GI	SERV	UM	CARB	FIBRE	GL
B194	Bread/Spec.	White wheat flour bread, homemade, frozen, defrosted	54	30	g	13		7
B200	Bread/Spec.	White wheat flour bread with added wheatgerm and fiber with oat fiber (UK) (Italy)	59	30	g	12		6
B193	Bread/Spec.	White wheat flour bread, frozen, defrosted and toasted, British Bakeries Ltd, (UK)	64	30	g	12		8
B229	Bread/Spec.	White bread, prepared with a 30 min prove and a second 12 min proving moderate loaf volume (UK)	72	30	g	13		9
B191	Bread/Spec.	White wheat flour bread, frozen and defrosted British Bakeries Ltd, (UK)	75	30	g	12		9
B230	Bread/Spec.	White bread, prepared with a 60 min prove and a second 30 min proving moderate loaf volume (UK)	86	30	g	13		11
B231	Bread/Spec.	White bread, prepared with a 40 min prove, a second 25 min proving and a third 50 min proving large loaf volume (UK)	100	30	g	13		13
B192	Bread/Spec.	White wheat flour bread, homemade, frozen and defrosted (UK)	62	30	g	13		8
B474	Cereal	Breakfast Cereal bar, hazelnut flavor (UK)	33	30	g	11		4
B475	Cereal	Breakfast Cereal bar, orange flavor (UK)	33	30	g	14		5
B473	Cereal	Breakfast Cereal bar, cranberry flavor (UK)	42	30	g	15		6
B312	Cereal	Bran cereal, high fiber (UK)	43	30	g	12		5
B313	Cereal	Branflakes, Healthy Living, (UK)	50	30	g	20		10
B342	Cereal	High-fiber cereal (UK)	52	30	g	17		9
B355	Cereal	Muesli, Alpen original, made from steamed rolled oats with dried fruit and nuts, Weetabix,	55	30	g	19		11

CATEGORY

REF#	CATEGORY	FOOD	GI	SERV	UM	CARB	FIBRE	GL
		(UK)						
B376	Cereal	Muesli, wholewheat (UK)	56	30	g	18		10
B363	Cereal	Muesli, fruit and nut (UK)	59	30	g	18		11
B353	Cereal	Mini Wheats, whole wheat, Sainsbury's, (UK)	59	30	g	21		12
B332	Cereal	Fruit and Fibre™, Sainsbury's, UK)	61	30	g	21		13
B397	Cereal	Porridge, organic, made from rolled oats (UK)	63	250	g	29		18
B396	Cereal	Porridge made from rolled oats, Value, UK)	63	250	g	30		19
B398	Cereal	Porridge, made from rolled oats, Scottish (UK)	63	250	g	31		20
B359	Cereal	Muesli, Value, UK)	64	30	g	19		12
B334.1	Cereal	Fruit and Fibre, mean of three studies	65	30	g	21		13
B333	Cereal	Fruit and Fibre (UK)	67	30	g	21		14
B362	Cereal	Muesli, fruit (UK)	67	30	g	21		14
B334	Cereal	Fruit and Fibre, Value, (UK)	68	30	g	20		13
B441	Cereal	Wheat based cereal biscuit (UK) (Plain flaked wheat)	72	30	g	20		14
B304	Cereal	Balance™, Sainsbury's, (UK)	74	30	g	23		17
B411	Cereal	Porridge, Instant oat cereal porridge prepared with water (UK)	83	250	g	36		30
B361	Cereal	Muesli, Healthy Eating, (UK)	86	30	g	21		18
B325	Cereal	Cornflakes, Kellogg's, (UK)	93	30	g	25		23
B458	Cereal/Spec.	Hot oat cereal 30 g, orchard fruit flavor (UK) prepared with 125 mL skim milk	5	155	g	25		12
B465	Cereal/Spec.	Porridge, jumbo oats (UK)Sainsbury's, UK), consumed with semi-skimmed milk	40	250	g	22		9
B455	Cereal/Spec.	Hot oat cereal, 30 g, cocoa flavor (UK) prepared with 125 mL skim milk	40	155	g	23		9

CATEGORY

REF#	CATEGORY	FOOD	GI	SERV	UM	CARB	FIBRE	GL
B460	Cereal/Spec.	Hot oat cereal, 30 g prepared with 125 mL skim milk (UK)	40	155	g	23		9
B454	Cereal/Spec.	Hot oat cereal 30 g, berry flavor (UK) prepared with 125 mL skim milk	43	155	g	26		11
B460.1	Cereal/Spec.	Cereal, Hot oat cereal mean of seven foods prepared with 125 mL skim milk	46	155	g	24		11
B469	Cereal/Spec.	Wheat Cereal biscuit 30 g, cocoa flavor, consumed with 125 mL skim milk (UK)	46	155	g	27		12
B459	Cereal/Spec.	Hot oat cereal 30 g prepared with 125 mL skim milk	47	155	g	23		11
B456	Cereal/Spec.	Hot oat cereal, 30 g, fruit flavor (UK) prepared with 125 mL skim milk	47	155	g	25		12
B457	Cereal/Spec.	Hot oat cereal, 30 g, honey flavor (UK), prepared with 125 mL skim milk	47	155	g	26		12
B472	Cereal/Spec.	Wheat Cereal biscuit 30 g, wheat based, consumed with 125 mL skim milk (UK)	47	155	g	26		12
B464	Cereal/Spec.	Muesli, Wheat free, Pertwee Farm's, (UK), consumed with semi-skimmed milk	49	30	g	19		9
B472.1	Cereal/Spec.	Wheat Cereal biscuit, consumed with 125 mL skim milk, mean of four foods	50	155	g	27		13
B471	Cereal/Spec.	Wheat Cereal biscuit 30 g, honey flavor, consumed with 125 mL skim milk (UK)	52	155	g	27		14
B453	Cereal/Spec.	Honey Crunch cereal 30 g, consumed with 125 mL skim milk (UK)	54	155	g	30		16
B470	Cereal/Spec.	Wheat Cereal biscuit 30 g, fruit flavor, consumed with 125 mL skim milk (UK)	56	155	g	27		15

CATEGORY

REF#	CATEGORY	FOOD	GI	SERV	UM	CARB	FIBRE	GL
B450	Cereal/Spec.	Cereal flakes with fruit (UK)30 g), consumed with 125 mL skim milk (UK)UK)	57	155	g	29		16
B451	Cereal/Spec.	Cocoa Crunch cereal 30 g with 125 mL skim milk (UK)	58	155	g	28		16
B467	Cereal/Spec.	Precise, Sainsbury's, (UK), with semi-skimmed milk	59	30	g	24		14
B462	Cereal/Spec.	Muesli, Original, Sainsbury's, (UK), consumed with semi-skimmed milk	60	30	g	19		11
B463	Cereal/Spec.	Muesli, Swiss, Sainsbury's, (UK), consumed with semi-skimmed milk	60	30	g	19		12
B466	Cereal/Spec.	Porridge, small oats, Sainsbury's, (UK), consumed with semi-skimmed milk	61	250	g	22		14
B452	Cereal/Spec.	Cornflakes, Sainsbury's, (UK) 30 g, consumed with 125 mL skim milk	65	30	g	25		16
B449	Cereal/Spec.	Branflakes, Sainsbury's, (UK), with semi-skimmed milk	76	30	g	20		15
B468	Cereal/Spec.	Rice Pops™, Sainsbury's, (UK), with semi-skimmed milk	80	30	g	25		20
B1180	Con. Meal	Cannelloni, spinach and ricotta (UK)	15	300	g	54		8
B1210	Con. Meal	Lasagne, vegetarian (UK)	20	300	g	48		10
B1216	Con. Meal	Lasagne, Pasta bake, tomato and mozzarella (UK)	23	300	g	43		10
B1209	Con. Meal	Lasagne, type NS (UK)	25	300	g	30		8
B1214	Con. Meal	Lasagne, Mushroom stroganoff with rice (UK)	26	300	g	43		11
B1207	Con. Meal	Lasagne, meat, Healthy Living, chilled, (UK)	28	300	g	38		11
B1196	Con. Meal	Cumberland pie (UK)	29	300	g	37		11
B1208	Con. Meal	Lasagne, type NS, Finest, (UK)	34	300	g	31		10
B1185	Con. Meal	Chicken tikka masala and rice, convenience	34	300	g	60		21

CATEGORY

REF#	CATEGORY	FOOD	GI	SERV	UM	CARB	FIBRE	GL
		meal, Healthy Living, (UK)						
B1205	Con. Meal	Lamb moussaka, prepared convenience meal, Finest, (UK)	35	300	g	27		10
B1195	Con. Meal	Cumberland fish pie (UK)	40	300	g	31		12
B1257	Con. Meal	Sweet and sour chicken with noodles, prepared convenience meal, Serves One, (UK)	41	300	g	52		21
B1200	Con. Meal	Fajitas, chicken (UK)	42	300	g	42		18
B1186	Con. Meal	Chilli beef noodles, prepared convenience meal, Finest, (UK)	42	300	g	46		19
B1181	Con. Meal	Chicken korma and peshwari rice, prepared meal,Finest, UK)	44	300	g	48		21
B1182	Con. Meal	Chicken korma and rice, convenience meal, Healthy Living, (UK)	45	300	g	48		21
B1258	Con. Meal	Tandoori chicken masala & rice convenience meal, Finest, (UK)	45	300	g	61		27
B1206	Con. Meal	Lasagne, beef, frozen (UK)	47	300	g	35		17
B1189	Con. Meal	Chow mein, chicken, convenience meal, Serves One, (UK)	47	300	g	38		18
B1253	Con. Meal	Steak and ale with cheddar mash potato convenience meal, Finest, (UK)	48	300	g	26		12
B1173	Con. Meal	Beef and ale casserole, convenience meal Finest, (UK)	53	300	g	15		8
B1188	Con. Meal	Chow mein, chicken, convenience meal, Healthy Living, (UK)	55	300	g	23		13
B1249	Con. Meal	Sausages and mash potato, prepared convenience meal (UK)	61	300	g	40		25
B1194	Con. Meal	Cottage pie (UK)	65	300	g	34		22
B1251	Con. Meal	Shepherds pie, prepared convenience meal (UK)	66	300	g	44		29
G/USDA	Dairy	Creamed cottage cheese	30	226	g	4	0	1

CATEGORY

REF#	CATEGORY	FOOD	GI	SERV	UM	CARB	FIBRE	GL
B758	Dairy	Fromage Frais, yellow fruit: passionfruit and pineapple, Healthy Living, (UK)	18	100	g	7		1
B756	Dairy	Fromage Frais, yellow fruit: mandarin and orange, Healthy Living, (UK)	19	100	g	7		1
B752	Dairy	Fromage Frais, red fruit: blackcurrant Healthy Living, (UK)	22	100	g	7		2
B759	Dairy	Fromage Frais, yellow fruit: peach and apricot, Healthy Living, (UK)	22	100	g	7		1
B754	Dairy	Fromage Frais, red fruit: red cherry (UK)Healthy Living,	25	100	g	7		2
B757	Dairy	Fromage Frais, yellow fruit: mango and papaya, Healthy Living, (UK)	25	100	g	7		2
B796	Dairy	Milk, semi-skimmed, British Dairycrest, (UK)	25	250	mL	13		3
B750	Dairy	Crème fraiche dessert, peach, Finest, (UK)	28	150	g	23		7
B755	Dairy	Fromage Frais, red fruit: strawberry, Healthy Living, (UK)	29	100	g	7		2
B751	Dairy	Crème fraiche dessert, raspberry, Finest, (UK)	30	150	g	17		5
B753	Dairy	Fromage Frais, red fruit: raspberryHealthy Living, (UK)	31	100	g	13		2
B787	Dairy	Milk, Full-fat, pasteurised, fresh, organic, Arla, (UK)	34	250	mL	12		4
B797	Dairy	Milk, semi-skimmed, pasteurised, organic Arla, (UK)	34	250	mL	13		4
B789	Dairy	Milk, Full-fat, standardised homogenised, pasteurised, British Dairycrest, (UK)	46	250	mL	12		5
B818	Dairy	Milk, skimmed, pasteurised, British Dairycrest, (UK)	48	250	mL	13		6
B859	Dairy/Yoghurt	Yoghurt, summer fruit: apricot, Healthy Living Light, (UK)	11	200	g	13		1

CATEGORY

REF#	CATEGORY	FOOD	GI	SERV	UM	CARB	FIBRE	GL
B842	Dairy/Yoghurt	Yoghurt, black cherry, Finest, (UK)	17	200	g	14		2
B864	Dairy/Yoghurt	Yoghurt, tropical fruit: guava and passionfruit, Healthy Living Light, (UK)	24	200	g	12		3
B860	Dairy/Yoghurt	Yoghurt, summer fruit: peach and vanilla, Healthy Living Light, (UK)	26	200	g	13		3
B866	Dairy/Yoghurt	Yoghurt, tropical fruit: peach and apricot, Healthy Living Light, (UK)	27	200	g	13		3
B861	Dairy/Yoghurt	Yoghurt, summer fruit: raspberry, Healthy Living Light, (UK)	28	200	g	12		3
B850	Dairy/Yoghurt	Yoghurt, peach & apricot, Healthy Living Light, (UK)	28	200	g	17		5
B857	Dairy/Yoghurt	Yoghurt, strawberry, Healthy Living Light, (UK)	30	200	g	16		5
B920	Dairy/Yoghurt	Yoghurt, Probiotic drink, orange (UK)	30	250	mL	34		10
B865	Dairy/Yoghurt	Yoghurt, tropical fruit: mango, Healthy Living Light, (UK)	32	200	g	13		4
B856	Dairy/Yoghurt	Yoghurt, Scottish raspberry, Finest, (UK)	32	200	g	40		13
B885	Dairy/Yoghurt	Yoghurt, Low-fat, raspberry (UK)	34	200	g	28		10
B921	Dairy/Yoghurt	Yoghurt, Probiotic drink, original (UK)	34	250	mL	31		11
B868	Dairy/Yoghurt	Yoghurt, Valencia orange, Finest, (UK)	34	200	g	33		11
B853	Dairy/Yoghurt	Yoghurt, red fruit: Morello cherry, Healthy Living Light, (UK)	35	200	g	12		4
B895	Dairy/Yoghurt	Yoghurt, low fat, natural (UK)	35	200	g	35		12
B862	Dairy/Yoghurt	Yoghurt, summer fruit: strawberry, Healthy Living Light, (UK)	36	200	g	13		5
B847	Dairy/Yoghurt	Yoghurt, Greek style, honey topped (UK)	36	200	g	32		12
B854	Dairy/Yoghurt	Yoghurt, red fruit: raspberry and black cherry, Healthy Living	37	200	g	13		5

CATEGORY

REF#	CATEGORY	FOOD	GI	SERV	UM	CARB	FIBRE	GL
		Light, (UK)						
B846	Dairy/Yoghurt	Yoghurt, Devonshire fudge, Finest, (UK)	37	200	g	34		13
B867	Dairy/Yoghurt	Yoghurt, tropical pineapple, Healthy Living Light, (UK)	38	200	g	13		5
B863	Dairy/Yoghurt	Yoghurt, toffee, Healthy Living Light, (UK)	41	200	g	16		7
B882	Dairy/Yoghurt	Yoghurt, Low-fat, black cherry (UK)	41	200	g	28		11
B858	Dairy/Yoghurt	Yoghurt, strawberry and cream, Finest, (UK)	41	200	g	38		16
B855	Dairy/Yoghurt	Yoghurt, red fruit: raspberry and cranberry, Healthy Living Light, (UK)	42	200	g	27		11
B881	Dairy/Yoghurt	Yoghurt, Low-fat, apricot (UK)	42	200	g	28		12
B849	Dairy/Yoghurt	Yoghurt, orange blossom, Finest, (UK)	42	200	g	40		17
B852	Dairy/Yoghurt	Yoghurt, raspberry, Healthy Living Light, (UK)	43	200	g	16		7
B908	Dairy/Yoghurt	Yoghurt, probiotic, prune (UK)	44	200	g	29		13
B909	Dairy/Yoghurt	Yoghurt, probiotic, raspberry (UK)	45	200	g	29		13
B869	Dairy/Yoghurt	Yoghurt, vanilla, Healthy Living Light, (UK)	47	200	g	14		7
B910.1	Dairy/Yoghurt	Yoghurt, probiotic, mean of three foods	47	200	g	29		14
B845	Dairy/Yoghurt	Yoghurt, champagne rhubarb, Finest, (UK)	49	200	g	38		19
B910	Dairy/Yoghurt	Yoghurt, probiotic, strawberry (UK)	52	200	g	29		15
B883	Dairy/Yoghurt	Yoghurt, Low-fat, hazelnut (UK)	53	200	g	29		15
B870	Dairy/Yoghurt	Yoghurt, white peach, Finest, (UK)	54	200	g	32		17
B884	Dairy/Yoghurt	Yoghurt, Low-fat, peach melba, Value, (UK)	56	200	g	28		16
B919	Dairy/Yoghurt	Yoghurt, Probiotic drink, cranberry (UK)	56	250	mL	31		17
B851	Dairy/Yoghurt	Yoghurt, peach melba, Value, (UK)	57	200	g	32		18
B886	Dairy/Yoghurt	Yoghurt, Low-fat, strawberry (UK)	61	200	g	30		18

CATEGORY

REF#	CATEGORY	FOOD	GI	SERV	UM	CARB	FIBRE	GL
B844	Dairy/Yoghurt	Yoghurt, bourbon vanilla, Finest, (UK)	64	200	g	32		20
B843	Dairy/Yoghurt	Yoghurt, black cherry, Healthy Living Light, (UK)	67	200	g	12		8
B848	Dairy/Yoghurt	Yoghurt, lemon curd, Finest, (UK)	67	200	g	45		30
B630	Digestive	Digestives (UK)	39	25	g	16		6
A318	Digestive	Digestives gluten-free, maize starch, Nutricia Dietary Care Ltd Redish Stockport (UK)	58	25	g	17		10
G/USDA/#	Fruit	Figs	40	28	g	8	1	3
G/USDA/#	Fruit	Cantaloupe	40	120	g	10	1	4
G/USDA/#	Fruit	Honeydew	40	120	g	11	1	4
G/USDA/#	Fruit	Strawberries	40	120	g	3	2	1
G/USDA/#	Fruit	Rhubarb	40	120	g	5	2	2
G/USDA/#	Fruit	Mulberries	40	120	g	12	2	5
G/USDA/#	Fruit	Apricot	40	120	g	13	2	5
G/USDA/#	Fruit	Papaya	40	120	g	13	2	5
G/USDA/#	Fruit	Plum	40	120	g	13	2	5
G/USDA/#	Fruit	Cherries, red	40	120	g	14	2	6
G/USDA/#	Fruit	Pineapple	40	120	g	16	2	3
G/USDA/#	Fruit	Mandarin	40	120	g	16	2	7
G/USDA/#	Fruit	Tangerine	40	120	g	16	2	7
G/USDA/#	Fruit	Mango	40	120	g	18	2	7
G/USDA/#	Fruit	Lychee	40	120	g	20	2	4
G/USDA	Fruit	Blueberries	29	120	g	17	3	5
G/USDA/#	Fruit	Plantain	40	120	g	38	3	10

CATEGORY

REF#	CATEGORY	FOOD	GI	SERV	UM	CARB	FIBRE	GL
G/USDA	Fruit	Banana, slightly under-ripe, yellow with green sections	42	120	g	25	3	11
G/USDA/#	Fruit	Blackberries	0	120	g	12	4	0
G/USDA/#	Fruit	Kiwi	40	120	g	18	4	6
G/USDA/#	Fruit	Soursop	40	120	g	20	4	2
G/USDA/#	Fruit	Persimmon	40	120	g	41	4	4
G/USDA/#	Fruit	Boysenberries	40	120	g	14	6	0
G/USDA/#	Fruit	Cranberries	40	120	g	14	6	6
G/USDA/#	Fruit	Guava	40	120	g	17	6	7
G/USDA/#	Fruit	Rose hips	40	28	g	11	7	4
G/USDA	Fruit	Avocado	0	120	g	11	8	0
G/USDA	Fruit	Raspberries	0	120	g	15	8	3
G/USDA/#	Fruit	Pomegranate	40	120	g	23	9	2
USDA/#	Fruit	Passionfruit	40	120	g	28	12	5
B951	Fruit	Apricots, dried, ready to eat (UK)	31	60	g	22		7
B952	Fruit	Apricots, dried, ready to eat, bite size (UK)	32	60	g	22		7
B1008	Fruit	Peach, dried (UK)	35	60	g	22		8
B1012	Fruit	Pear, dried (UK)	43	60	g	27		12
B1030	Fruit	Sultanas, Value, (UK)	56	60	g	42		23
B1031	Fruit	Sultanas (UK)	58	60	g	42		24
B992	Fruit	Mixed fruit, dried, Value, (UK)	60	60	g	41		24
B492	Grain	Barley, pearled, boiled 60 min (UK)	35	150	g	42		15
B557	Grain	Rice, Basmati, white, boiled, Sainsbury's, (UK)	43	150	g	43		18
B532	Grain	Rice, American, easy-cook rice, Sainsbury's, (UK)	49	150	g	46		22

REF#	CATEGORY	FOOD	GI	SERV	UM	CARB	FIBRE	GL
B524	Grain	Long grain, white, pre-cooked, microwaved 2 min, Express Rice, plain, Uncle Ben's, Masterfoods, (UK)	52	150	g	37		19
A280	Grain	Long grain white precooked microwaved 2 min, Express Rice plain Uncle Ben's; King's Lynn Norfolk (UK)	52	150	g	37		19
B565	Grain	Rice, Precooked basmati rice in pouch, white, reheated in microwave, Uncle Ben's Express® Masterfoods, (UK)	57	150	g	41		24
A297	Grain	Precooked basmati rice in pouch white reheated in microwave, Uncle Ben's Express; Masterfoods. Kings Lynn Norfolk (UK)	57	150	g	41		24
B564	Grain	Rice, Basmati, easy-cook rice, boiled, Sainsbury's, (UK)	68	150	g	41		28
B558	Grain/Spec.	Rice, Basmati, white, boiled 12 min, Value, (UK)	52	150	g	28		15
B558	Grain/Spec.	Rice, Basmati, white, boiled 12 min, Value, (UK)	52	150	g	28		15
B559	Grain/Spec.	Rice, Basmati, white, organic, boiled 10 min (UK)	57	150	g	40		23
B563	Grain/Spec.	Rice, Basmati, easy cook, white, boiled 9 min (UK)	67	150	g	42		28
B562	Grain/Spec.	Rice, Basmati, white, boiled 8 min (UK)	69	150	g	40		28
B1066	Infant Foods	Apple, apricot and banana cereal, Robinsons first Tastes from 4 months, Nutricia, Wells, (UK)	56	75	g	13		7
A447.1	Infant foods	Apple apricot and banana cereal6, Robinsons First Tastes from 4 months, Nutricia Wells, (UK)	56	75	g	13		11

CATEGORY

REF#	CATEGORY	FOOD	GI	SERV	UM	CARB	FIBRE	GL
B1067	Infant Foods	Creamed rice porridge, Robinsons first Tastes from 4 months, Nutricia, Wells, (UK)	59	75	g	9		5
A447.2	Infant foods	Creamed porridge, Robinsons First Tastes from 4 months, Nutricia Wells (UK)	59	75	g	9		5
B1068	Infant Foods	Rice pudding, Robinsons first Tastes from 4 months, Nutricia, Wells, (UK)	59	75	g	11		6
A447.3	Infant foods	Rice pudding, Robinsons First Tastes from 4 months (Nutricia Wells UK)	59	75	g	11		6
B1153	Meal Repl. & Weight Mgmt.	SlimFast® Garden vegetable soup with peppers and croutons, SlimFast Foods Ltd, UK)	20	250	mL	27		5
B1131	Meal Repl. & Weight Mgmt.	Chocolate weight management drink (UK)	23	250	mL	18		4
B1149	Meal Repl. & Weight Mgmt.	SlimFast® chocolate meal replacement bar SlimFast Foods Ltd, UK)	27	50	g	23		6
B1129	Meal Repl. & Weight Mgmt.	Chocolate, lactose-free, weight management drink (UK)	29	250	mL	19		6
B1146	Meal Repl. & Weight Mgmt.	Lemon weight management bar (UK)	32	50	g	21		7
B1152	Meal Repl. & Weight Mgmt.	SlimFast® Strawberry Supreme ready-to-drink shake, SlimFast Foods Ltd, UK)	33	250	mL	30		10
B1151	Meal Repl. & Weight Mgmt.	SlimFast® Double Chocolate meal replacement powder, prepared with skim milk, SlimFast Foods Ltd, UK)	36	50	g	46		17
B1132	Meal Repl. & Weight Mgmt.	Chocolate weight management drink (UK)	39	250	mL	18		7
B1147	Meal Repl. & Weight Mgmt.	Malt toffee weight management bar (UK)	43	50	g	24		10
B1150	Meal Repl. & Weight Mgmt.	SlimFast® Chocolate Muesli snack bar, SlimFast Foods Ltd, UK)	49	50	g	32		16
B1154	Meal Repl. & Weight Mgmt.	SlimFast® Pasta Florentina meal,	53	250	g	34		12

CATEGORY

REF#	CATEGORY	FOOD	GI	SERV	UM	CARB	FIBRE	GL
		SlimFast Foods, UK)						
B1148	Meal Repl. & Weight Mgmt.	SlimFast® chocolate caramel meal replacement bar, SlimFast Foods Ltd, Slough, Berks, UK)	54	50	g	33		18
G/USDA	Meat, Fish & Poultry	All meat, fish, shellfish, poultry, including wild game or meats	0			0	0	0
G/USDA	Nuts	Macadamia	0	50	g	7	4	0
G/USDA	Nuts	Walnuts	0	50	g	7	4	0
G/USDA	Nuts	Pecans	0	50	g	7	5	0
G/USDA	Nuts	Hazelnuts	0	50	g	8	5	0
G/USDA	Nuts	Almond meal flour	0	50	g	11	6	0
G/USDA	Nuts	Almonds	0	50	g	11	6	0
B1322	Nuts	Mixed nuts and raisins (UK)	21	50	g	16		3
B1323	Nuts	Mixed nuts, roasted and salted (UK)	24	50	g	17		4
B1318	Nuts	Cashew nuts (UK)	25	50	g	12		3
B1319	Nuts	Cashew nuts, organic, roasted and salted (UK)	25	50	g	12		3
B1320	Nuts	Cashew nut halves (UK)	27	50	g	10		3
B1321	Nuts	Cashew nuts, roasted and salted (UK)	27	50	g	10		3
B1383	Pasta	Tagliatelle, egg pasta, boiled in water for 7 min (UK)	46	180	g	44		20
B1333	Pasta	Fusilli pasta twists, tricolour, dry pasta, boiled 10 min in unsalted water (UK)	51	180	g	45		23
B1343	Pasta	Lasagne, egg, verdi, dry pasta, boiled in unsalted water for 10 min (UK)	52	180	g	45		23
B1342	Pasta	Lasagne, egg, dry pasta, boiled in unsalted water for 10 min(UK)	53	180	g	43		23
B1343.1	Pasta	Lasagne, egg, verdi, boiled in unsalted water	53	180	g	45		24

CATEGORY

REF#	CATEGORY	FOOD	GI	SERV	UM	CARB	FIBRE	GL
		for 10 min, mean of three studies						
B1335	Pasta	Gluten-free pasta, maize starch, boiled 8 min (UK)	54	180	g	42		23
A522	Pasta	Gluten-free pasta maize starch boiled 8 min (UK)	54	180	g	42		22
B1384	Pasta	Tagliatelle, egg, boiled, Sainsbury's, UK)	54	180	g	44		24
B1332	Pasta	Fusilli pasta twists, dry pasta, boiled in 10 min in unsalted water (UK)	54	180	g	48		26
B1334	Pasta	Fusilli pasta twists, wholewheat, dry pasta, boiled 10 min in unsalted water (UK)	55	180	g	41		23
B1334.1	Pasta	Fusilli pasta, twists, mean of four studies	55	180	g	46		25
B1341	Pasta	Lasagne sheets, dry pasta, boiled in unsalted water for 10 min, Value, UK)	55	180	g	47		26
B1331	Pasta	Fusilli pasta twists, Tesco Stores Ltd, UK), boiled 10 min in salted water (UK)	61	180	g	48		29
B1218	Pasta/Spec.	Fusilli pasta twists, Tesco Stores Ltd, UK), boiled 10 min in salted water, served with cheddar cheese (UK)	27			48		13
B1217	Pasta/Spec.	Fusilli pasta twists, Tesco Stores Ltd, UK), boiled 10 min in salted water, served with canned tuna (UK)	28			48		13
B1219	Pasta/Spec.	Fusilli pasta twists, Tesco Stores Ltd, UK), boiled 10 min in salted water, served with chilli con carne (UK)	40			48		19
USDA/#	Pulses	Cocoa powder, unsweetened	40	5	g	3	1	1
USDA/#	Pulses	Carob powder, unsweetened	40	6	g	5	2	2
G/USDA	Pulses	Chickpea (Garbanzo Bean) flour	10	30	g	18	5	2
B1115	Pulses	Lentils, red, split, dried,	21	150	g	18		4

CATEGORY

REF#	CATEGORY	FOOD	GI	SERV	UM	CARB	FIBRE	GL
		boiled 25 min (UK)						
B1128	Pulses	Split peas, yellow, dried, soaked overnight, boiled 55 min (UK)	25	150	g	13		3
B1090	Pulses	Butter Beans, dried, soaked overnight, boiled 50 min (UK)	26	150	g	20		5
B1111	Pulses	Red Kidney Beans, dried, soaked overnight, boiled 60 min (UK)	51	150	g	24		12
G/USDA	Snack	Sardines, fish snacks, canned	0	95	g	0	0	0
G/USDA	Snack	Egg, hardboiled	0		g	1	0	0
G/USDA	Snack	Dill Pickle	40	28	g	0.6	0.3	0
H/USDA	Snack	Hummus, chickpea salad dip, commercially prepared	6	30	g	4	2	0
G/USDA	Snack	Celery with Cashew Butter	40	80	g	10	2	2
G/USDA	Snack	Celery with Hummus	40	80	g	7	3	0
H/USDA	Snack	Microwave popcorn plain, average	55	20	g	11	3	6
G/USDA	Snack	Apple slices with peanut butter	38	120	g	23	5	9
G/USDA	Snack	Apple slices with peanut butter	38	120	g	23	5	9
G/USDA	Snack	Chocolado Parfait with a Cherry, (From recipe in Are You Sweet Enough Already?)	40	113	g	12	6	5
B1410	Snack	Fruit and nut mix, Finest, UK)	15	50	g	24		4
B1412	Snack	Apricot and Almond bar (UK)	34	30	g	15		5
B743	Snack	Crackers, Wholewheat with pumpkin and thyme (UK)UK)	36	25	g	15		6
B716	Snack	Crackers, Choice grain (UK)	49	25	g	16		8
B1499	Snack	Tropical fruit and nut mix, Finest, UK)	49	50	g	28		14
B744	Snack	Crackers, Wholewheat sticks, crunchy, yeast extract flavored (UK)	50	25	g	14		7

CATEGORY

REF#	CATEGORY	FOOD	GI	SERV	UM	CARB	FIBRE	GL
B742	Snack	Crackers, Wholegrain with sesame seeds and rosemary (UK)	53	25	g	16		8
B734	Snack	Crackers, Rye with sesame (UK)	57	25	g	16		9
B733	Snack	Crackers, Rye with oats (UK)	64	25	g	16		10
B1543	Soup	Garden vegetable soup with peppers and croutons, SlimFast®, SlimFast Foods Ltd, Slough, Berks, UK)	20	250	g	27		5
B1540	Soup	Chicken and mushroom soup (UK)	46	250	g	18		8
B1557	Soup	Vegetable soup (UK)	60	250	g	18		11
B1541	Soup	Chicken and mushroom soup (UK)	69	250	g	19		13
A744/USDA	South American	Corn tortilla (Mexican)	52	50	g	24	1	12
A749/USDA	South American	Wheat tortilla (Mexican)	30	50	g	26	5	8
PKG	Sweetener	Stevia extract	0			0	0	0
PKG	Sweetener	Stevia extract	0			0	0	0
PKG	Sweetener	Stevia	0	1	g	<1	0	0
PKG	Sweetener	Xylitol (1 packet)	7	2.04	g	2	0	0
PKG	Sweetener	Coconut palm sugar	35	4	g	4	0	1
PKG	Sweetener	Coconut palm sugar	35	4	g	4	0	1
PKG	Sweetener	Blackstrap molasses	55	15	mL	13	0	7
A591.2	Sweetener	25 g Litesse III ultra bulking agent with polydextrose and sorbitol, (by weight), Danisco Sweeteners UK) vs 25 g carb in ref food (glucose).	4	10	g	10		0
A591.1	Sweetener	25 g Litesse II bulking agent with polydextrose and sorbitol (by weight), Danisco Sweeteners UK) vs 25 g. carb in ref food (glucose).	7	10	g	10		1
A593.3	Sweetener	25 g Xylitol (by weight), Danisco Sweeteners UK) vs ref food (glucose) with 25 g. carb. Mean of 2 studies	8	10	g	10		1
B1599	Sweetener	Lactose, 25 g portion,	48	10	g	10		5

CATEGORY

REF#	CATEGORY	FOOD	GI	SERV	UM	CARB	FIBRE	GL
		DBH, Poole, (UK)						
G/USDA	Vegetable	Radish	40	30	g	1	1	0
G/USDA	Vegetable	Watercress	40	120	g	2	1	1
G/USDA	Vegetable	Cucumber	40	120	g	4	1	2
G/USDA	Vegetable	Mushrooms	40	120	g	4	1	2
G/USDA	Vegetable	Zucchini	40	120	g	4	1	2
G/USDA	Vegetable	Ginger root	40	28	g	5	1	2
G/USDA	Vegetable	Radiccio	40	120	g	5	1	2
G/USDA	Vegetable	Tomato	40	120	g	5	1	2
G/USDA	Vegetable	Bok Choy	40	120	g	7	1	3
G/USDA	Vegetable	Garlic	40	28	g	8	1	3
G/USDA	Vegetable	Green Leaf Lettuce	0	150	g	4	2	0
G/USDA	Vegetable	Arugula	40	120	g	4	2	2
G/USDA	Vegetable	Celery	40	120	g	4	2	2
G/USDA	Vegetable	Swiss chard	40	120	g	4	2	2
G/USDA	Vegetable	Cauliflower	40	120	g	6	2	2
G/USDA	Vegetable	Tomatillo	40	120	g	7	2	3
G/USDA	Vegetable	Bell pepper	40	120	g	11	2	4
G/USDA	Vegetable	Kale	40	120	g	11	2	4
G/USDA	Vegetable	Onion	40	120	g	11	2	4
G/USDA	Vegetable	Leek	40	120	g	17	2	7
G/USDA	Vegetable	Spinach	0	150	g	4	3	0
G/USDA	Vegetable	Asparagus	40	120	g	5	3	2

CATEGORY

REF#	CATEGORY	FOOD	GI	SERV	UM	CARB	FIBRE	GL
G/USDA	Vegetable	Cabbage	40	120	g	7	3	3
G/USDA	Vegetable	Broccoli	40	120	g	8	3	3
G/USDA	Vegetable	Beet greens	40	120	g	12	3	5
G/USDA	Vegetable	Eggplant	40	120	g	7	4	3
G/USDA	Vegetable	Kohlrabi	40	120	g	7	4	3
G/USDA/#	Vegetable	Olives	40	120	g	7	4	3
G/USDA	Vegetable	Green Beans	40	120	g	8	4	3
G/USDA	Vegetable	Okra	40	120	g	8	4	3
G/USDA	Vegetable	Dandelion greens	40	120	g	11	4	4
G/USDA	Vegetable	Collard greens	40	120	g	6	5	2
G/USDA	Vegetable	Jicama	40	120	g	11	6	4
G/USDA	Vegetable	Artichoke	40	120	g	13	6	5
G/USDA	Vegetable	Turmeric root	40	28	g	18	6	7
G/USDA	Vegetable	Grape leaves	40	60	g	10	7	4
G/USDA	Vegetable	Wheatgrass	40	30	g	16	8	6
G/USDA	Vegetable	Mustard greens	40	120	g	7	9	3
B1640	Vegetable	Potato, Marfona, peeled, quartered, boiled 15 min in unsalted water (UK)UK)	56	150	g	32		18
B1642	Vegetable	Potato, Nicola, peeled, quartered, boiled 15 min (UK)	59	150	g	16		9
B1634	Vegetable	Potato, Charlotte, peeled, quartered, boiled 15 min (UK)	66	150	g	23		15
B1637	Vegetable	Potato, Estima, peeled, quartered, boiled 15 min (UK)	66	150	g	26		17
B1627	Vegetable	Potato, white, baked with skin, baked (UK)	69	150	g	27		19

CATEGORY

REF#	CATEGORY	FOOD	GI	SERV	UM	CARB	FIBRE	GL
B1639	Vegetable	Potato, King Edward potato, peeled, quartered, boiled 15 min in unsalted water (UK)	75	150	g	28		21
B1680	Vegetable	Potato, New, boiled (UK)	80	150	g	23		18
B1635	Vegetable	Potato, Charlotte, boiled (UK)	81	150	g	23		19
B1641	Vegetable	Potato, Maris Piper, peeled, quartered, boiled 15 min in unsalted water (UK)	85	150	g	29		25
B1674	Vegetable	Potato, Estima, microwaved 6 min then baked 10 min (UK)	93	150	g	26		24
B1651	Vegetable	Potato, white, boiled (UK)	96	150	g	26		24
B1630	Vegetable	Potato, white, baked without skin, baked (UK)	98	150	g	27		26
B1672	Vegetable	Potato, Desiree, mashed (UK)	102	150	g	26		26
B1654	Vegetable/Spec.	Potato, Type NS, boiled in salted water, refrigerated, reheated, India)	23	150	g	34		8
B1228	Vegetable/Spec.	Potato, Estima, 50 g, microwaved 6 min then baked 10 min, served with cheddar cheese 62 g (UK)	39	112	g	26		10
B1226	Vegetable/Spec.	Potato, Estima, 50 g, microwaved 6 min then baked 10 min, served with baked beans, 89 g, (UK)	62	139	g	37		23
B1229	Vegetable/Spec.	Potato, Estima 50 g, microwaved 6 min then baked 10 min, served with chilli con carne, 63 g (UK)	75	113	g	31		23
B1227	Vegetable/Spec.	Potato, Estima, 50 g, microwaved 6 min then baked 10 min, served with canned tuna, 62 g (UK)	76	112	g	26		20

ENDNOTES, REFERENCES, & RESOURCES

ENDNOTES, REFERENCES & RESOURCES:

In all of the lists, the first column is "Ref #." This is the published reference number which refers to the source of information presented. More than one reference is used in many cases. A "/" separates multiple resources.

Here are the information resources used in the preparation of these collections:

- "A" = International Tables of Glycemic Index and Glycemic Load Values, 2002. This research is archived by the US National Library of Medicine, National Institutes of Health The individual tables of glycemic study results are available at: https://www.ncbi.nlm.nih.gov/pubmed/12081815 This table contains nearly 1,300 study results from countries all over the world. The exact number of the study result in the table is also included in the charts of *CHEAT SHEET Simply for UK Foods* for your convenience.

- "B" = International Tables of Glycemic Index and Glycemic Load Values, 2008. Here is the entire article: https://www.ncbi.nlm.nih.gov/pmc/articles/PMC2584181/ This research is archived by the US National Library of Medicine, National Institutes of Health The individual tables of glycemic study results are available at: https://www.ncbi.nlm.nih.gov/pmc/articles/PMC2584181/bin/dc08-1239_index.html. These tables contain 2,478 of these individual food study results from countries all over the world. The exact number of the study result is referenced in the charts of *CHEAT SHEET Simply for UK Foods* for your convenience.

- "G" = Glycemicindex.com. http://www.glycemicindex.com/

- "H" = Harvard University: http://www.health.harvard.edu/diseases-and-conditions/glycemic_index_and_glycemic_load_for_100_foods

- "USDA" = USDA National Nutrient Database for Standard Reference is a listing of 8,789 foods. The United States Department of Agriculture database provides information *in CHEAT SHEET SIMPLY FOR UK FOODS* regarding fibre content and carbohydrate in cases of calculating glycemic load. https://ndb.nal.usda.gov/ndb/

- "PKG" = Portions of nutritional information is provided from the product packaging.

- "#" = Only 8 dried UNITED KINGDOM OF GREAT BRITAIN fruits have been tested for their glycemic values. Therefore, fruits lacking a lab-tested glycemic index test score are given a

ENDNOTES, REFERENCES, & RESOURCES

---

value based on a simple mathematic calculation. A total of all tested fruits' GI scores for the USA Edition (found in *Cheat Sheet Simply for USA Foods*, were added together and divided by the total number of tested fruit scores. There are 22 fruits with lab-tested scores, the total of their scores adding up to 870. 870 divided by the 22 fruits = 39.55. This was done to verify the accuracy of Glycemic Index "assignment." Assignment is done because eating 50g carbohydrate portions of many foods may not be humanly possible in order to conduct testing. Since a fruit is part of a vegetable, and any untested vegetable is assigned a GI score of 40, any untested fruits are therefore assigned a GI value of 40.

- For other works by this author please see: amazon.com/author/judylickus

- Learn more details about using carb counts, glycemic index, and glycemic load at the informative blog: LowGlycemicHappiness.com

- Like us on Facebook at: Facebook.com/Low Glycemic Happiness.

- For 120 recipes for blood sugar control, please see *Low Glycemic Happiness*, available in paperback and EBook formats at Amazon, bookstores, and libraries. Each of the recipes (and snacks) in this book uncommonly show the carbohydrate, glycemic index, fiber, glycemic load, plus other nutrition details (calories, fat, saturated fat, protein, and sodium content) per serving.

- For the top 10 low glycemic load dessert recipes for blood sugar control, please see *Are You Sweet Enough Already?*, available in paperback and EBook formats at Amazon, bookstores, and libraries. A few of the dessert recipes are included in the charts of this book because they use less common dessert recipe ingredients, like black beans, avocado, and almond flour. These recipes contain no high glycemic flour or table sugar products. You will also see the amount of carbohydrate, glycemic index, fiber, glycemic load, plus other nutrition details (calories, fat, saturated fat, protein, and sodium content) per serving.

ENDNOTES, REFERENCES, & RESOURCES

MY NOTES ON CARBOHYDRATE

ENDNOTES, REFERENCES, & RESOURCES

MY NOTES ON CARBOHYDRATE

ENDNOTES, REFERENCES, & RESOURCES

MY NOTES ON GLYCEMIC INDEX

ENDNOTES, REFERENCES, & RESOURCES

MY NOTES ON GLYCEMIC INDEX

ENDNOTES, REFERENCES, & RESOURCES

MY NOTES ON FIBRE

ENDNOTES, REFERENCES, & RESOURCES

MY NOTES ON FIBRE

ENDNOTES, REFERENCES, & RESOURCES

MY NOTES ON GLYCEMIC LOAD

ENDNOTES, REFERENCES, & RESOURCES

MY NOTES ON GLYCEMIC LOAD

ENDNOTES, REFERENCES, & RESOURCES

MY NOTES ON FOOD CATEGORIES

ENDNOTES, REFERENCES, & RESOURCES

MY NOTES ON FOOD CATEGORIES

ENDNOTES, REFERENCES, & RESOURCES

ENDNOTES, REFERENCES, & RESOURCES

Printed in Great Britain
by Amazon